D0507036

Rocco's Real Life Recipes
fast flavor for every day

Meredith® Books
Des Moines, Iowa

ROCCO DISPIRITO

Meredith Books
1716 Locust Street
Des Moines, Iowa 50309–3023
meredithbooks.com

Printed in the United States of America.

First Edition.
Library of Congress Control Number: 2007921722
ISBN: 978-0-696-23703-4

contents

4   introduction

6   look and cook

8   the perfect pantry

10   techniques

16   beef

48   poultry

98   pork

120   lamb

132   salmon

146   tuna

162   shellfish

200   Rocco's Reserve

230   index

Introduction
Real life.
It's getting up, getting the kids to school, staying at work later than you want to, being away from home for 10 hours and then getting home exhausted at the end of the day and wanting to pick up the phone and call for delivery pizza—every night of the week.

Eating is something we all have to do to fuel us through that real life. Unfortunately, eating microwave meals or takeout every night does not contribute to the good life. A big part of the good life is sitting down and enjoying a great meal with people you love. That's what this book is all about—helping you make real life the good life.

I took the best of all my experiences—the flavor combinations I cultivated as a chef, the dishes my mom invented that I grew up eating, and quick and easy recipes and cooking techniques—and synthesized them in this book.

I feel like I have a unique experience. Since I left the restaurant business, the challenges of cooking at home have become more real to me. I have a typical New York City apartment kitchen. I don't have sous chefs like I used to, and I don't have dishwashers like I used to. It's just me, and I still have to eat, and I still love to have family and friends over for dinner. This book is a great solution to all of the problems the home cook faces every weeknight. It is built completely around how we want to cook and eat. With the exception of the recipes in the Reserve chapter (if you want to challenge yourself or do some leisurely weekend cooking), every recipe in this book:

Uses everyday ingredients. I didn't go to a single gourmet store or farmer's market in creating these recipes. I shopped and researched at regular grocery stores, tasted, catalogued, and created lists of everyday ingredients, and from those I created these recipes.

Uses minimal ingredients. It's easy to get overwhelmed with shopping, chopping, and measuring when you want to get dinner on the table, pronto. Most of these recipes have just 8 to 10 ingredients (or fewer), including salt and pepper.

Has a short cooking time. Including prep time, you can have dinner on the table in 20 to 30 minutes, with time and energy to spare.

Strategically combines fresh foods and high-quality shortcut foods. I believe in putting good, fresh food in your body—and I also believe that taking advantage of all of the great prepared foods out there is a no-brainer.

Is built on a most-popular protein. When most people think about what to make for dinner, they think first about the protein. Chicken or fish? Beef or pork? The recipes in this book are based on solid research into what Americans are eating.

Is an entrée. I know from personal experience that most people are focused on cooking entrées. So instead of taking up half of the book with recipes for chocolate panna cotta and pâté, I wanted to offer what was most useful. Add a salad and a glass of wine to any recipe in this book, and you'll be very happy.

Makes minimal mess. The last thing you want to do after a great meal is clean up a big pile of pots and pans. Any time I could make a recipe in one pan, I did.

Is easy to use. In addition to the inherent usability of the recipes, there are some extra tools to help you plan your meal making (see "Look and Cook," page 6, for more information on those).

Tastes fabulous. Anyone who knows me as a chef knows that I think flavor is the most important thing when it comes to enjoying food. These are not plain old dishes. They all have some interesting flavor combinations. The combination may not be something you've seen before, but with one bite the taste is familiar.

There isn't a person in the world you can't win over by cooking something and sitting down and eating with them. Why not do it more often and as much as you possibly can?

Look and Cook

At 5 p.m. on any given weekday, a simple recipe is a beautiful thing—but it's not necessarily everything you need to get dinner on the table by 6:30. That's where a couple of additional helps I've included in this book come in. Here's how they work:

A grocery list

that accompanies every recipe tells you just what you need to make that recipe. To make list making and shopping even easier, I've broken down the ingredients into three categories so at a glance you can figure out what you already have and what you need. (See "The Perfect Pantry," page 8.)

Fresh

This is pretty much anything you can get behind the counter that's not usually packaged in a factory. This includes produce—vegetables, fruits, most fresh herbs, and salad greens—meat, poultry, fish and shellfish, and fresh or short-storing cheeses.

Packaged

This can be anything in a bag, box, can, carton, jar, or bottle. It includes dry pastas, rice, pasta sauces, more exotic condiments, bagged salad, and so on.

Staples

This also can be anything in a bag, box, can, carton, jar, or bottle —but it's also something you use over and over again and in lots of different recipes. Staples include salt and pepper, dried herbs and spices, oils and vinegars, butter, eggs, lemons and limes, chicken broth, and long-storing cheeses such as Parmigiano-Reggiano.

A tools bar

shows you the primary cooking vessel or vessels you need to make the recipe. This is not only so you can see if you have that pan, but also what you're going to have to wash (not much). I kept mess to a minimum by choosing ingredients that don't require a lot of prep, and I didn't include any exotic equipment in this book—so more than likely you have everything you need to make every recipe in it. (If you don't have a large sauté pan—or two—or a very large saucepan, you might want to invest in them.) When I call for a grill/grill pan/broiler, choose what you prefer. I put them in that order because I think cooking on a grill is easiest, fastest, and brings out the greatest flavor. A grill pan is not something everyone has, but it's a good alternative to the grill. And then the broiler. The success of certain recipes depends on it. There's nothing like a blast of top heat to make a cheesy casserole brown and bubbly.

A wine guide

that starts on page 204 helps you pair what I consider high quality, good value wines with the foods you love to eat.

less than 30 minutes

Tools

2 large skillets

large saucepan

Grocery List

Fresh

1½ pounds beef tenderloin
1 bunch chives

Packaged

5-ounce package garlic and herb Boursin® cheese
2 16-ounce packages Alexia® frozen mashed potatoes
10-ounce package frozen peas
1 pint heavy cream

Staples

extra-virgin olive oil

The Perfect Pantry

A well-stocked pantry is the key to making quick, flavorful meals. And by pantry, I don't just mean the cabinet where you keep your Wheaties. The pantry includes that cereal-storing space as well as your refrigerator, freezer, and countertop.
Here's some staple stuff you should always have around.

Good Things to Have In Your Fridge/Freezer

Butter
Eggs
Milk
Cream
Parmigiano-Reggiano cheese
Other assorted cheeses
Salad greens
Fresh herbs (flat-leaf parsley is the most versatile)
Gravlax or smoked salmon
Favorite proteins: sirloin, strip steak, lamb chops, pork chops, chicken cutlets/boneless, skinless breasts, skinned and filleted salmon, peeled and deveined shrimp
Green and yellow vegetables: fresh broccoli rabe, bagged baby spinach, green beans, asparagus, carrots, frozen green peas
Olives
Apples, Pears, Lemons, Limes, Oranges

Good Things to Have on Your Countertop

Onions
Head of fresh garlic
Fresh tomatoes
Idaho potatoes

Condiments & Sweeteners

Dijon mustard, Chinese mustard
Wasabi
Horseradish
Ketchup
Mayonnaise
Salsa
Peanut butter
Peanut sauce
Curry paste
Soy sauce
Capers
Anchovies
Miso paste
Marmalade (orange, grapefruit, lemon)
Honey
Maple syrup
Applesauce
Mirin

Dry Goods

All-purpose flour
Granulated sugar, brown sugar
Cornmeal
Breadcrumbs (seasoned and plain)
Dried pasta (spaghetti, orzo, pastina, etc.)
Rice
Instant polenta
Nuts (walnuts, almonds, peanuts)
Loose-leaf black tea

Canned Goods

Beans (white, black, pinto, kidney)
Tomatoes (peeled whole plum tomatoes/crushed tomatoes)
High-quality soups
Chicken broth
Tuna, packed in oil
Roasted red peppers
Pasta sauce (marinara, puttanesca, etc.)
Coconut milk

Oils & Vinegars

Bertolli® extra-virgin olive oil
Cooking oil (canola, corn, etc.)
Red wine vinegar, white wine vinegar, balsamic vinegar, rice wine vinegar

Seasonings & Spices

Fine salt
Sea salt
Peppercorns (white and black, for freshly ground)
Nutmeg
Allspice
Cumin
Chili powder
Crushed red pepper
Curry powder
Mustard powder
Paprika
Dried thyme
Dried oregano
Dried rosemary
Sesame seeds

Miscellaneous

Wine (your favorite dry red and white)

Techniques

Ironically, my culinary training and years of experience as a chef have taught me that there isn't one right way to do things in the kitchen. The right way is your way. There are, though, some tips and techniques that are good to know to make the process of cooking as enjoyable as it can be and the food that comes from it as delicious as it can be. Here are a few basics.

prepping avocados

Put the avocado in the palm of your hand and, using a large chef's knife, cut lengthwise into the fruit. Turn the avocado all of the way around so the knife glides through, cutting the fruit in half horizontally.

Twist the avocado halves apart so the flesh and seed are exposed.

With a quick, slightly forceful chopping motion bring the blade down onto the seed so the blade sticks into it. Turn the knife about a quarter turn and slowly lift up, pulling the seed up and out of the fruit.

To get the flesh of the avocado out of the skin, pinch each half, rolling the skin back and forth until all of the flesh is removed. Squeeze a little fresh lemon juice over the avocado flesh to keep its vibrant green color.

making chicken cutlets

Slice the chicken breast lengthwise so the cutlet is about ½ inch thick. Use the weight of your hand against the top of the cutlet to guide the knife through cleanly.

After cutting in a few inches, pull the sliced part of the chicken back to fan out the cutlet as you continue to slice. Repeat the previous step to create several cutlets as needed.

mincing chives

Dampen a paper towel and fold it into thirds lengthwise. Place your chives across the short width of the paper towel and create a tight bundle. Roll the chives with the paper towel into a firm bundle with 2 inches left exposed.

Cut off about 1 inch of the exposed chives, then cut the bundled chives very finely. Move the paper towel as you work your way back through the bundle until the whole bunch is chopped.

chopping parsley

Start with a large bundle of parsley and a sharp knife.

Remove the stems and discard, leaving only the leaves of the parsley. Gather the leaves in your non-dominant hand and place your fist on the cutting board, exposing a little of the leaves at a time as you chop.

Keeping your fingers curled, let your hand move backwards, letting go of more parsley as the knife moves forward chopping it. Let the flat side of the knife rest against your knuckles as you cut, using them—not your fingertips—as the guide.

cutting on a bias

Cutting on a bias literally means to cut diagonally across the grain of something.

Cutting on a bias means to cut on an angle; It makes foods like scallions or carrots look a little prettier. Place a few scallions on a cutting board. Hold your knife at a 45° angle across the top of them and begin slicing.

The result you get isn't tubular but a little bit pointed—like penne pasta. Continue slicing through, adjusting the angle of your knife to determine just how angled you would like the pieces to be.

prepping garlic

Choose bulbs of garlic that are firm and plump and have papery dry skin.

Smash the head of garlic with a good amount of force so that it falls apart, exposing all of the cloves. Remove the excess papery skin from the head, leaving only the individual cloves with their skin still on.

Place the flat side of your knife on top of a single clove, and bring your palm down on top of the knife in a quick motion to crush the clove. Peel the skin and discard, leaving only the cloves for use.

slicing London broil

When cut correctly, cheaper cuts of meats can be tender and delicious.

The grain of the meat is the direction that the fibers of the muscle run. In a piece of flank steak (like the one shown here), the grain is obvious and creates very thin indentations in the meat.

Holding the knife at a 45° angle, slice through in one fluid motion, pulling the knife toward you as you go. Continue on an angle, slicing each piece about ¼ inch thick.

heating oil

When you cook with oil in a skillet or sauté pan, there are a few crucial steps you need to take and visual cues to watch for that will give you great results every time.

Always heat your pan first before you pour in the oil. Heating it first makes the surface hot enough to create an instant crust on the food. This makes it release easily from the pan rather than sticking.

When the oil begins to heat, it will become thinner and looser, and you'll be able to swirl it around the bottom of the pan.

When it's close to a high temperature, the oil will become clearer and have a shimmer to it. Always use oil with a high flash or smoke point such as light olive oil, vegetable oil, or safflower oil.

When the oil reaches the highest temperature in which it's still safe to cook, it will be very fluid and smoking. This is the last step before the flash point where the oil decomposes, loses its flavor, and is dangerously hot.

sweating onions

Sweating is the process of creating flavor with moisture and a very low cooking temperature. To get the best flavor, sweating with butter is the best technique.

Sweating sweetens flavors by using moisture and a very low cooking temperature. Heat a saucepan over low heat and slowly melt 2 tablespoons of unsalted butter until it dissolves.

Carefully add a large, chopped onion to the pan. Season with salt and pepper and stir the onion with a wooden spoon to evenly coat all of it with butter.

Cover the chopped onion with a tight lid and let the steam create condensation.

Gently cook the onion for about 10 minutes or until translucent and tender, stirring it every 2 minutes.

Perfect grilling technique

Grilling is one of my favorite ways to cook. It's generally healthful, you get great-looking markings on the food, and it only requires a little olive oil, salt, and pepper to get fabulous flavor. There are just a few basic steps to take for perfect grilling results every time. Here's how to perfectly grill boneless center loin pork chops. Except for the final internal temperature—which varies according to what you're cooking—the same technique applies to any kind of meat.

Start with a hot, clean, and dry grill pan (although the rest of this technique applies to cooking on an outdoor grill, too).
Brush each pork chop with a small amount of olive oil on one side.

Sprinkle the oiled sides with a mixture of salt and freshly cracked pepper.

Add each pork chop to the grill with the grate lines going horizontal to the length of the chop. Leave the chops alone for 2 minutes so the grill marks develop nicely. Using a pair of tongs, turn the chops a quarter-turn so they lay at the opposite angle of the grate lines.

Using a dry dishcloth or paper towel, blot the top of the meat as condensation collects.

Brush the exposed sides with olive oil.

Add another sprinkle of salt and some fresh cracked pepper.

For ¾ inch thick chops, allow 3 to 4 minutes per side, then turn.

Allow another 3 to 4 minutes to cook or until internal temperature reaches 160° F.

levels of doneness in meat
Before learning how to test the doneness of your meat, it's important to know how you like to eat it.

testing doneness in meat
The best way to check, is to compare the way the cooked meat feels to the way the flesh of your hand feels.

Rare
A reddish, cool-to-warm center that's soft and spongy, with an internal temperature of about 120°F

Rare
Press the fleshy part of your palm on the opposite hand. The relaxed muscle is soft and yielding and resembles a rare piece of meat.

Medium Rare
A warm, red center with a springy firmness and an internal temperature of about 125°F

Medium Rare
A bent pointer finger will give you a comparable feel of medium rare when you press on that same muscle.

Medium
A hot pink center with a very slightly springy firmness and an internal temperature of about 135°F

Medium
A bent middle finger will give you the feel of medium doneness (very slightly springy).

Medium Well
Very slight pink color throughout and a firm feel, with an internal temperature of about 145°F

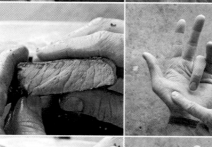

Medium Well
A bent ring finger will tighten the muscle further and feel slightly firm, like medium well.

Well done
No pink color left with a very firm feel with an internal temperature of about 160°F

Well done
The muscle is completely taut when you bend your pinky finger, which gives you the same feel as a well-done piece of meat.

B E E F

"The easiest way to get someone to fall in love with you is to feed them."

Giada

Filet Mignon with Cheese and Potatoes

No need to be a snob. I found great prepared potatoes and I love frozen peas. If it's good, it's good. The sweet and salty Boursin® cheese packs a 1-2 flavor punch in a single ingredient, and the fresh chives add a great taste that only just-picked herbs can offer. –R

Tools

2 large skillets

large saucepan

Grocery List

Fresh

1½ pounds beef tenderloin
1 bunch chives

Packaged

5-ounce package garlic and herb Boursin® cheese
2 16-ounce packages Alexia® frozen mashed potatoes
10-ounce package frozen peas
1 pint heavy cream

Staples

extra-virgin olive oil

1. Heat a large skillet over high heat.

2. Heat the potatoes according to package directions. Transfer the potatoes to the large saucepan. Add the cheese and mash the mixture roughly with a potato masher or large fork. Toss in the peas and heat through. Season to taste with salt and pepper.

3. Meanwhile, in the other skillet heat the oil. Dry or blot the beef with paper towels, then season well with salt and pepper. Carefully lay beef in the hot pan and sear it for about 2½ minutes per side. (The beef will stick to the skillet until it's ready to be turned.) Remove the beef from skillet when doneness is to your liking. Add the cream and the 1 tablespoon pepper to the skillet. Bring to a slight boil and reduce by half.

4. Divide potatoes among four plates. Place beef on top of the potato mixture and add the cream mixture; sprinkle chives over the top and serve.

Serves 4

2   16-ounce packages Alexia® frozen mashed potatoes
1   5-ounce package garlic and herb Boursin® cheese
2   cups frozen peas
    Salt and freshly ground pepper
2   tablespoons Bertolli® extra virgin olive oil
1½ pounds beef tenderloin, cut into four 6-ounce portions
1½ cups heavy cream
1   tablespoon freshly ground pepper
1   bunch fresh chives, chopped

Beef Minute Steak
with Sour Cherry-Mustard Glaze

Cherries and mustard may sound odd, but they're so good together. There's an Italian condiment called *mostarda*, which is fruit preserved in syrup with mustard seed—so it's a classic pairing. I've tried many fruit-and-mustard combinations—this is my favorite. —R

Serves 4

¼ cup red wine vinegar
¼ cup water
½ cup red wine
½ cup dried sour cherries
½ cup sugar
1 tablespoon strong
     Dijon mustard
     Salt and freshly
       ground pepper
2 pounds top-round
     minute steak
3 medium red onions,
     peeled and cut into
     ½-inch-thick rings

1. Preheat a grill/grill pan/broiler over high heat.

2. In a medium saucepan combine red wine vinegar, water, red wine, sour cherries, and sugar. Bring mixture to a boil. Turn off the heat and let the cherries rest for 3 minutes. Puree by pulsing cherries in a blender or food processor. Stir in mustard and season to taste with salt and pepper.

3. Reserve ½ cup of the cherry mixture. Place remaining cherry mixture in a large mixing bowl. Season the beef with salt and pepper. Add the onions to the mixing bowl. Toss to coat evenly. Place the onions on the cooking surface and cook over very high heat for 1 minute. Add the beef to the mixing bowl. Toss to coat evenly and add to the onions. Cook beef and onions turning the beef once, until the onions and beef are cooked to your liking, about 1 minute per side for rare.

4. Drizzle reserved glaze over the meat and serve steaks with onions.

Tools

grill pan

medium saucepan
blender/food processor

Grocery List

Fresh

2 pounds top-round minute
steak
3 medium red onions

Packaged

8-ounce package dried sour
cherries

Staples

red wine vinegar
red wine/sugar
Dijon mustard

Sirloin Steak with Kale and Mustard

Kale is so underappreciated. Its flavor is rich, it has great texture, and it's incredibly good for you. When I saw this Cut 'n Clean Greens™ product in the stores, I was thrilled. Who wants to spend time washing sand out of anything? –R

Tools

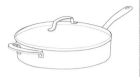

large sauté pan

Grocery List

Fresh

8 thin sirloin steaks
(about 1½ pounds)

Packaged

1-pound package Cut 'n Clean
Greens™ kale

Staples

cooking oil/chicken broth
red wine
Dijon mustard/flour

1. Heat a large sauté pan over high heat. Add the oil and let it get very hot (it will begin to smoke). Place the flour in a shallow dish. Dredge steaks in flour and shake off the excess. When the oil is shimmering and almost smoking, add half of the steaks. Cook 1 minute per side for rare and 2 minutes per side for well done. Remove steaks from the pan and season with salt and pepper. Keep warm near the stove top and repeat with remaining steaks.

2. Drain all but 1 tablespoon of the oil from the pan and lower the heat to medium. Add the kale and quickly sauté until it turns dark green and tender. Pour in the red wine and the chicken broth. Use a wooden spoon to scrape up any flavorful steak bits from the bottom of the pan. Increase the heat to high and simmer the sauce until it reduces by half, 2 to 3 minutes. Whisk in the Dijon mustard. Season to taste with salt and pepper.

3. Transfer steaks to a serving platter and spoon the kale with pan sauce over the top.

Serves 4

¾ cup cooking oil

3 cups all-purpose flour

8 thin sirloin steaks, about
   1½ pounds
   Salt and freshly ground
   pepper

1 pound package Cut 'n
   Clean Greens™ kale, or
   1 bunch fresh kale,
   washed well and chopped

1 cup red wine

1 cup chicken broth

4 tablespoons Dijon
   mustard

Pepper Steak in a Flash

I used to eat Chinese food a lot as a kid. Even my very Italian mom would come with me once a week to enjoy all the wonderful dishes of the great Chinese kitchen. The only one that baffled us was "pepper steak." It was never good—this version is much better. –R

Serves 4

- 4   8-ounce flat-iron steaks
       Salt
- 2   tablespoons coarse-ground black pepper
- 4   tablespoons Bertolli® extra-virgin olive oil
- 1   12-ounce jar Mancini® roasted red peppers
- 2   12-ounce jars Mancini® fried peppers
- 1   19-ounce jar Heinz® home-style pork gravy

1. Heat a large sauté pan over high heat. Season the steaks with salt. Sprinkle coarse pepper over each of the steaks on both sides, pressing the pepper into the meat with the heel of your palm.

2. Add 2 tablespoons of the oil to the pan and let it get hot. Add half of the steaks to the pan and sear until brown, about 2 minutes per side. Remove the steaks from pan. Repeat with remaining oil and half of steaks.

3. Add peppers and gravy to the pan and bring to a boil. Add the steaks back to the pan, reduce to a simmer, and finish cooking the steaks in the pepper mix until medium rare, about 5 minutes. Spoon peppers and sauce over steaks to serve.

Tools

large sauté pan

Grocery List

Fresh

4 8-ounce flat iron steaks

Packaged

12-ounce jar Mancini® roasted red peppers
2 12-ounce jars Mancini® fried peppers
19-ounce jar Heinz® homestyle pork gravy

Staples

extra-virgin olive oil

less than 15
minutes

Horseradish-and-Cinnamon-Marinated
Skirt Steak with Pears and Scallions

What's skirt steak? It's called "skirt" steak because it comes from the place (on the animal) where you'd wear a skirt. Funny, huh? Bottom line: It's delicious and inexpensive. And did you know that horseradish and fruits like apple and pears taste great together? –R

Tools

broiler pan

Grocery List

Fresh

1½- to 1¾-pounds skirt steak
4 large Anjou pears
1 bunch scallions

Packaged

6-ounce jar prepared horseradish
12-ounce jar apple jelly

Staples

apple cider vinegar
ground cinnamon
extra-virgin olive oil

1. In a medium bowl, mix the horseradish into the apple jelly. Stir in 2 tablespoons of the vinegar and the cinnamon. Completely coat the steaks in this marinade, cover, and refrigerate for 9 hours or overnight.

2. Prepare the grill by wiping it down with a paper towel soaked in a little olive oil. This will create a nonstick surface. Heat the grill to high. (You may also use a broiler pan under the broiler.)

3. Season the steaks well with salt and pepper and, depending on thickness, grill or broil for about 1½ to 2 minutes per side. Remove the steaks to a clean platter and allow to rest while you prepare the rest of the dish.

4. Toss the pears, scallions, 2 tablespoons olive oil, and remaining 2 tablespoons of cider vinegar in a medium bowl. Season pear salad with salt and pepper and make a pile in the center of a serving platter. Slice steak against the grain, if desired, and arrange on top of the pears.

Serves 4

½ cup prepared horseradish
1 cup apple jelly
4 tablespoons apple cider vinegar
½ teaspoon ground cinnamon
1½- to 1¾-pounds skirt steak
 Salt and freshly ground pepper
4 large ripe Anjou pears, sliced thin
1 large bunch scallions, cut on a diagonal
2 tablespoons Bertolli® extra-virgin olive oil, plus extra for grill

See photos, pages 68-69.

Marmalade-Marinated **Flank Steak** with Glazed Carrots

I created this for *Good Morning America* on Memorial Day some years ago. Back then I focused on labor-intensive dishes using expensive ingredients. The producer wisely asked me to come up with something simple for the first weekend of summer. –R

Serves 4

- 1   12-ounce jar orange marmalade, English if possible
- ½   cup red wine vinegar
- 1   tablespoon chili powder
- ½   cup ketchup
- 2   tablespoons Dijon mustard
- 1   tablespoon Worcestershire sauce
- 2   pounds flank steak
      Salt and freshly ground pepper
- 1   10-ounce bag Dole® carrot slaw

1. In a large bowl, combine all ingredients except the steak, the salt and pepper, and the slaw. Whisk to combine. Set aside 1 cup of the marinade. Add the flank steak to the remaining marinade and coat well. Cover and refrigerate overnight.

2. In a small saucepan, boil the reserved marinade with the carrot slaw for 5 minutes, or until thickened to a glaze consistency.

3. Preheat a grill/grill pan/broiler on high. When your pan or grill is very hot, remove the steak from the marinade and season both sides with salt and pepper. Grill until medium-rare, about 3 minutes on each side. Let the steak rest for 5 minutes.

4. To serve, thinly slice the steak against the grain. Serve steak with the glazed carrot slaw.

Tools

small saucepan

grill pan

Grocery List

Fresh

2 pounds flank steak

Packaged

12-ounce jar orange marmalade
5-ounce bottle Worcestershire sauce
10-ounce bag Dole® carrot slaw

Staples

red wine vinegar
chili powder
ketchup/Dijon mustard

Flank Steak Forestière

À la forestière means "of the forest" in French. It usually refers to a dish that includes mushrooms and herbs—things that might be found in a forest. The French have a way of making everything sound so pretty *and* complicated—but this isn't complicated at all. –R

Tools

Dutch oven

Grocery List

Fresh

2 pounds flank steak
2 cups white button
mushrooms

Packaged

3.15-ounce Amore® tube garlic
paste
2 14.5-ounce cans whole
peeled plum tomatoes
1-ounce package fresh
tarragon

Staples

onion
red wine
dark brown sugar/butter

1. Preheat the oven to 350°F.

2. In a large Dutch oven, melt 2 tablespoons of the butter over medium heat until foaming. Season the flank steak on both sides with salt and pepper. Brown the steak in the butter, one piece at a time, about 2 to 3 minutes per side.

3. As each piece is browned, remove it to a clean plate. When all of the steak is browned, add the remaining tablespoon of butter to the pot, then the onion, garlic paste, and mushrooms. Season vegetables generously with salt and pepper and cook until softened, about 5 minutes, stirring occasionally. Add the brown sugar and stir until it melts.

4. Add the wine to the pot and bring it to a simmer. Cook, stirring occasionally, until all of the wine evaporates, about 5 minutes. Add the tomatoes and tarragon. Bring the mixture back up to a simmer and put the steak back into the pan. (The liquid should come halfway up the sides of the beef.) Cover the pot and transfer it to the oven to cook for 12 minutes.*

5. Remove the pan from the oven. Transfer the meat to a cutting board and let it rest for 5 minutes. (If the liquid looks too soupy, remove the beef from the pot and reduce the liquid over medium-high heat until it has thickened.) Slice the steak very thin and serve with sauce and vegetables.

✳ Cooking the flank steak more than 12 minutes will toughen it—and it will require braising in the oven for about another hour to make it tender again.

Serves 4

3 tablespoons butter
2 pounds flank steak, cut in three equal pieces
Salt and freshly ground pepper
1 onion, diced
2 tablespoons Amore® garlic paste, or 6 garlic cloves, chopped
2 cups white button mushrooms, quartered
3 tablespoons packed dark brown sugar
½ cup red wine
2 cups canned whole peeled plum tomatoes, drained and cut into quarters
4 tablespoons chopped fresh tarragon

See photo, page 70.

Medallions of Beef with Gingered Greens

Ginger is one of those exotic ingredients that's become mainstream. It has great health benefits and tastes like nothing else. Fresh ginger can hang around in your fridge for months. I use pureed ginger from a jar to streamline things. —R

Serves 4

- 4 tablespoons Bertolli® extra-virgin olive oil
- 8 4-ounce beef tenderloin fillets
  Salt and freshly ground pepper
- 1 cup fresh shiitake mushrooms, stems removed and discarded, caps sliced thin
- 3 tablepoons ginger puree
- 1 tablespoon Amore® garlic paste, or 3 garlic cloves chopped
- 1 bunch broccoli rabe, cleaned and cut into 3-inch long pieces
- ½ cup unsweetened coconut milk

1. In a large skillet, heat 2 tablespoons of the olive oil over high heat until oil is lightly smoking. Season fillets with salt and pepper. Add half of the fillets to the pan and sear until golden brown, about 1½ minutes per side for medium rare. Remove steaks to a clean plate and repeat with remaining steaks. Allow steaks to rest for 5 minutes.

2. Keep the pan hot on the stove. Add the remaining 2 tablespoons olive oil to the pan. Add the mushrooms and cook for 1 minute. Stir in the ginger and garlic and cook, stirring, for 2 minutes. Add the broccoli rabe and sauté until it begins to wilt, about 2 minutes. Add the coconut milk and simmer for 2 minutes. Season to taste with salt and pepper. Place 2 steaks on each of four plates. Spoon the sauce over the steaks.

Tools

large skillet

Grocery List

Fresh

8 4-ounce beef tenderloin fillets
1 cup shiitake mushrooms
1 bunch broccoli rabe

Packaged

7.5-ounce jar ginger puree
3.15-ounce Amore® tube garlic paste
14-ounce can unsweetened coconut milk

Staples

extra-virgin olive oil

Medallions of Beef with Crab and Squash Stew

I have long been a fan of mixing meat and fish. At first people react with trepidation until they're reminded of the dish they see at most banquets, weddings, and charity receptions—surf 'n' turf. The combo of crab and beef is already a classic. —R

Tools

large skillet

Grocery List

Fresh

8 4-ounce beef tenderloin fillets
8-ounce package white button mushrooms

Packaged

7.5-ounce jar ginger puree
16-ounce can crabmeat
16-ounce container Campbell's® Select™ butternut squash soup

Staples

extra-virgin olive oil
sour cream

1. In a large skillet heat 2 tablespoons of the olive oil over high heat until lightly smoking. Season fillets to taste with salt and pepper. Add half of the fillets to the pan and sear until golden brown, about 1½ minutes per side for medium rare. Remove steaks to a clean plate and repeat with remaining steaks. Allow steaks to rest for 5 minutes.

2. Keep the pan hot on the stove. Add the remaining 2 tablespoons olive oil to the pan. Add mushrooms and cook for 1 minute. Stir in the ginger and cook, stirring, for 2 minutes. Add the soup and crabmeat and bring to a boil. Reduce heat and simmer for 2 minutes. Whisk in the sour cream. Place 2 steaks in each of four large shallow bowls. Top steaks with crab stew.

Serves 4

4 tablespoons Bertolli® extra-virgin olive oil
8 4-ounce beef tenderloin fillets
Salt and freshly ground pepper
3 cups white button mushrooms, sliced
3 tablespoons ginger puree
1 cup Campbell's® Select™ golden butternut squash soup
1 16-ounce can pasteurized crabmeat
½ cup sour cream

Tenderloin of Beef
with Bacon, Squash, and Five-Spice Powder

less than 30 minutes

Butternut squash is very easy and quick to cook—especially when it's sold peeled and cut. (And there's no flavor sacrifice.) It's every bit as good as the more exotic varieties and is available most of the year. —R

Serves 4

- 8 pieces thick-cut sliced bacon, cut into ½-inch-wide strips
- 2 20-ounce packages precut butternut squash
- 2 tablespoons Chinese five-spice powder
- Salt and freshly ground pepper
- 4 6- to 8-ounce beef tenderloin medallions
- 2 4-ounce cans pear nectar
- 2 tablespoons chopped fresh flat-leaf parsley

1. Preheat the oven to 350°F.

2. Heat a large sauté pan over high heat. Add the bacon to the pan and cook for about 3 minutes. Remove the bacon from the pan, draining all but about 2 tablespoons of fat. Turn heat down to low while you get the squash ready for the oven.

3. Place bacon in a large mixing bowl. Toss squash with bacon and transfer it to a baking sheet. Cook the squash in the oven for about 20 minutes or until tender. Season with five-spice powder, salt, and pepper.

4. Meanwhile, turn the heat back up to high and season the beef on all sides with salt and pepper. Add beef to the pan and brown the meat, basting with the bacon fat as it cooks, about 5 minutes per side. Transfer the medallions to a rack or platter and let them rest while you make the pear sauce.

5. Pour out any excess fat from the pan. Over high heat, add the pear nectar to the pan, scraping up any bits of bacon or beef with a wooden spoon. Stir in the parsley. Serve the tenderloin alongside the vegetables, spooning the sauce over everything.

Tools

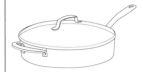

large sauté pan

Grocery List

Fresh

8 slices thick-cut bacon
4 6- to 8-ounce beef tenderloin medallions
1 bunch flat-leaf parsley

Packaged

2 20-ounce packages precut butternut squash
2 4-ounce cans pear nectar

Staples

five-spice powder

less than 15 minutes

Beef and Fried-Pepper Carpaccio

Some people think pepper steak is boring, but I love it. This 42-second version is simple, foolproof, and really good. —R

Tools

large nonstick skillet

1. Heat a large nonstick skillet over medium heat. Add half the olive oil and heat until hot but not smoking. Add the breadcrumbs and cook, stirring, until they turn golden brown. Add the peppers and capers and heat through. Stir in parsley; season with salt and pepper to taste.

2. To serve, divide the hot pepper mixture among four plates. Place one-quarter of the sliced roast beef in an overlapping circle on top of the peppers on each plate. Season with salt and pepper, and drizzle with remaining olive oil and lemon juice. Serve warm or at room temperature.

Serves 4

¼ cup Bertolli® extra-virgin olive oil, plus extra for drizzling

⅛ cup plain breadcrumbs

2 12-ounce jars of Mancini® fried peppers

3 tablespoons capers, rinsed and drained

½ cup flat-leaf parsley, chopped

Salt and freshly ground pepper

¾ pound fresh rare roast beef from the deli, sliced very thin

1 tablespoon fresh lemon juice

Grocery List

Fresh

1 bunch flat-leaf parsley
¾ pound rare deli roast beef

Packaged

2 12-ounce jars Mancini® fried peppers

Staples

plain breadcrumbs
capers/lemon juice
extra-virgin olive oil

Grilled **Beef Kabobs** with Eggplant and Orzo

If you don't want to fire up the grill, you can cook the kabobs under the broiler—or even on top of the stove on a grill pan. —R

Serves 4

- 2 lemons, juice and zest (finely grated) of both
- 2 teaspoons Amore® garlic paste or 2 cloves garlic, chopped
- ½ cup fresh flat-leaf parsley, chopped
- ½ cup Bertolli® extra-virgin olive oil, plus extra for drizzling
- 8 prepared beef kabobs
- 1½ cups orzo
  Salt and freshly ground pepper
- 2 cups prepared baba ganoush or eggplant caviar

1. In a medium bowl combine the lemon juice, garlic, ¼ cup parsley, and ½ cup of olive oil. Put the kabobs in a resealable plastic bag and pour the marinade over them. Seal the bag tight and marinate the kabobs in the refrigerator for at least 2 hours, but preferably overnight.

2. Preheat grill or broiler pan to medium-high. Meanwhile, in a large saucepan of salted water, cook the orzo according to package instructions. (Be sure to stir the orzo as it cooks, as it tends to stick to the bottom of the pot.) While the orzo is cooking, remove the kabobs from the marinade and season well with salt and pepper. Grill the kabobs for about 8 minutes for medium rare, or until desired doneness is achieved, turning occasionally so that each side is evenly cooked and browned.

3. Combine the cooked orzo with the lemon zest, remaining parsley, and enough of the eggplant mixture to generously coat and bind the orzo mixture. Season to taste with salt and pepper, if necessary. Drizzle orzo with extra-virgin olive oil and serve with the kabobs.

tip Zest the lemons before you juice them—then keep the finely grated zest under a moist paper towel until you're ready to add it to the orzo.

Tools

broiler pan

large saucepan

Grocery List

Fresh

8 beef kabobs
1 bunch flat-leaf parsley

Packaged

3.15-ounce Amore® tube garlic paste
2 7.5-ounce containers baba ganoush
1-pound package orzo

Staples

lemons
extra-virgin olive oil

Charred **Steak** with Mushroom Vinaigrette

When you blacken a steak by charring it on a cast-iron skillet or on a grill, you make it sweeter by converting protein into sugar. Enough chemistry, though—it just tastes really good. The sweet-and-sour mushrooms take this simple steak to a higher level. –R

Tools

2 large cast-iron skillets

large sauté pan

Grocery List

Fresh

1½ pounds mixed wild mushrooms
4 beef strip, ribeye or tenderloin steaks
1 bunch chives

Packaged

3.15-ounce Amore® tube garlic paste

Staples

extra-virgin olive oil
sherry vinegar
honey/butter

1. Preheat two large cast-iron skillets over high heat until extremely hot, about 5 minutes.

2. While the skillets are heating, make the mushroom mixture. Heat the olive oil in a very large sauté pan over high heat. Add the mushrooms and cook until they are a light golden brown color, stirring occasionally, about 4 minutes. Season the mushrooms with salt and pepper. Lower the heat to medium and add the garlic to the pan. Cook about 1 minute. Add the vinegar, honey, and butter to the pan. Stir in to create a creamy "vinaigrette." Keep warm over low heat.

3. Meanwhile, pat the steaks with a paper towel and season generously with salt and pepper. Place two steaks in each of the dry, hot skillets. Press down on them to make sure they are flush with the surface of the skillets. Cook until charred and very rare in the center, about 1½ to 2 minutes per side (or a little longer if you prefer your steaks more well done). Allow steaks to rest for a few minutes.

4. Stir the chopped chives into the mushrooms and liberally pile the mixture on top of the charred steaks.

Serves 4

3	tablespoons Bertolli® extra-virgin olive oil
1½	pounds mixed wild mushrooms, cut into bite-size pieces
	Salt and freshly ground pepper
2	teaspoons Amore® garlic paste or 2 garlic cloves, chopped
½	cup sherry vinegar
¼	teaspoon honey
8	tablespoons butter (1 stick)
4	beef strip or ribeye or tenderloin steaks, about 10 ounces each
4	tablespoons chopped fresh chives (about 1 bunch)

Boiled **Beef** and Pappardelle

Soups are a staple in Southeast Asia. In Vietnam they're called *pho*. They're served with condiments like chili sauce, fish sauce, and vinegar so you make your own flavor combo. I've simplified the process and used mustard to amp up the intensity of the broth. –R

Serves 4

8	cups chicken broth
1	pound fresh pappardelle (or any other fresh pasta noodle)
⅓	cup Dijon mustard
1	pound fresh rare roast beef from the deli, sliced very thin
½	cup thinly sliced green onions
	Salt and freshly ground pepper

See photo, page 71.

1. In a medium saucepan, bring chicken broth to a boil. Add pasta and simmer until fully cooked, about 4 minutes. Whisk in the mustard.

2. Cut the roast beef into 2-inch squares. Divide roast beef slices among four large soup bowls. Divide the pasta and broth equally among the bowls. Scatter the green onions on top. Season each serving with salt and pepper to taste and serve very hot.

Tools

medium saucepan

Grocery List

Fresh

1 pound rare deli roast beef
1 bunch green onions

Packaged

1 pound fresh pappardelle pasta

Staples

chicken broth
Dijon mustard

Chipped **Beef** with Rice Noodles and Chiles

When I was in Pittsburgh with my friend Tom Poljak, his mother served us "chipped" beef. I loved it. So even though this dish was created in her honor, other than the "chipped" (very thinly sliced) beef, nothing else is the same. You got to make it your own. —R

Tools

large saucepan

Grocery List

Fresh

2 cups bean sprouts
1 bunch cilantro
1¼ pounds shaved deli roast beef

Packaged

7-ounce package rice sticks
12-ounce can unsweetened coconut milk
7-ounce jar fish sauce
1-ounce package fresh mint

Staples

chicken broth
crushed red pepper

1. Soak rice noodles in water for 5 minutes.

2. In a large saucepan over high heat, combine chicken broth, coconut milk, fish sauce, and crushed red pepper. Bring to a boil. Add the rice noodles and bring to a boil again. Simmer until the noodles are tender, about 5 minutes. Season soup with salt and pepper to taste.

3. Meanwhile, divide the bean sprouts, mint, cilantro, and roast beef among four large soup bowls. Using a pair of tongs, lift the noodles from the broth and divide among the bowls. Ladle the hot coconut broth over the noodles, vegetables, and meat in each bowl and serve very hot.

Serves 4

- 4 ounces dry rice-stick noodles
- 4 14-ounce cans chicken broth
- 1 12-ounce can unsweetened coconut milk
- 2 tablespoons fish sauce
- 1 tablespoon crushed red pepper flakes
  Salt and freshly ground pepper
- 2 cups bean sprouts
- ½ cup fresh mint, chopped
- ½ cup fresh cilantro, chopped
- 1¼ pounds shaved deli roast beef

Quick **Beef** and Mushroom Stew

less than 30 minutes

Beef and mushrooms make great partners, and miso (a flavorful Japanese soybean paste) and mushrooms are sublime. I try to use miso as much as possible. –R

Serves 4

4 tablespoons Bertolli®
    extra-virgin olive oil
2 pounds cubed beef
    tenderloin tips or beef
    tenderloin, cut into large
    chunks
1 cup all-purpose flour
    Salt and freshly ground
    pepper
1 pound mixed mushrooms
    such as cremini,
    button, and/or shiitake
    mushrooms, stems
    removed, cut in half
4 teaspoons Amore®garlic
    paste or 4 garlic cloves,
    chopped
3 tablespoons tomato paste
1 cup red wine
1 cup chicken broth
1 bunch scallions, trimmed
    and cut on a diagonal
    Hot cooked rice (optional)

1. Heat 2 tablespoons of the oil in a heavy-bottomed Dutch oven over high heat. Season both the beef and flour with salt and pepper. Toss the beef in the flour and shake off any excess. When you see a slight smoke coming from the pot, carefully lay half of the beef in it, browning it quickly on all sides. Remove the beef from the pot and set aside; repeat with other half of the beef.

2. Heat the Dutch oven over very high heat again. Add another tablespoon of oil to the pot. Toss in the mushrooms and sauté them until soft, stirring occasionally, about 2 minutes. Add the remaining oil and garlic and sauté until fragrant, about 1 minute. Add the tomato paste. Cook and stir it for about 1 minute.

3. Pour in the red wine and stir, scraping up any flavorful brown bits, and simmer it until almost evaporated. Once the wine has reduced, add the chicken broth. Bring this mixture to a boil. Add the browned beef back to the pot; turn the heat down to bring the quick stew to a light and even simmer.

4. At this point, it might be ready to serve—or, if you like your meat well done, continue to simmer the stew until the meat is cooked to your liking. The longer you cook it, the thicker the sauce becomes and more well-done the meat becomes.

5. Season the stew with a good amount of freshly ground black pepper. Sprinkle the scallions on top and serve over rice, if you like.

tip For a variation, add 4 tablespoons light miso paste with the chicken broth and stir in 4 tablespoons rice wine vinegar before serving.

Tools

Dutch oven

Grocery List

Fresh

2 pounds beef tenderloin tips
or beef tenderloin
1 pound mixed mushrooms
1 bunch scallions

Packaged

3.15-ounce Amore® tube garlic
paste

Staples

extra-virgin olive oil
flour/ tomato paste
red wine/chicken broth

less than 15 minutes

Cold **Beef** and Italian Bread Salad

Deli roast beef is very versatile. It's a good way to get fresh-cooked beef on the table without spending more time than it takes to buy it. You can serve it cold or reheated in panini, pasta, or over rice with condiments like curry paste or harissa—a Tunisian hot sauce. —R

Tools

large skillet

Grocery List

Fresh

1 loaf Italian bread
1 pound thinly sliced deli roast beef
4 tomatoes

Packaged

1 pound fresh mozzarella
1-ounce package fresh basil

Staples

red wine vinegar
red onion
extra-virgin olive oil

1. Heat a skillet over medium-high heat until hot. Add the bread pieces and toast on all sides for about 3 to 4 minutes or until golden brown.

2. In a large bowl, toss toasted bread with vinegar until well combined.

3. Add beef, onion, tomatoes, and mozzarella. Gently toss mixture with the olive oil and season with salt and pepper to taste. Add torn basil just before serving.

4. Serve immediately or cover and refrigerate for up to 24 hours.

note If the salad is being refrigerated overnight, the basil should not be added until right before you serve it.

Serves 4

1   loaf fresh Italian bread, cut into bite-size chunks
¾   cup red wine vinegar
1   pound thinly sliced deli roast beef
1   red onion, sliced thin
4   ripe tomatoes, cut into bite-size chunks
1   pound fresh mozzarella, torn into bite-size chunks
½   cup Bertolli® extra-virgin olive oil
    Salt and freshly ground pepper
1   bunch fresh basil, torn

Hot and Sour **Beef** and Cabbage

less than 30
minutes

"Hot and sour"—a term usually applied to soup—refers here to the great flavor of this stir-fry. The combination of the beef, cabbage, and Thai curry sauce is exotic enough to be interesting but familiar enough to not challenge your taste buds too much. –R

Serves 4

3 tablespoons cooking oil

1½ pounds thinly sliced beef
 for stir-fry

Salt and freshly ground
 pepper

1 medium red onion, sliced
 thin

1 16-ounce package Dole®
 cabbage slaw

1 16-ounce package Mann's
 California Stir Fry®
 vegetables

1 cup Soy Vay® Veri Veri
 Teriyaki marinade

2 tablespoons Thai Kitchen®
 red curry paste

1. Heat a large sauté pan or wok over high heat. Add the oil to the pan and let the oil get very hot. When the oil is smoking, season the beef with salt and pepper. Stir-fry half of the beef for 3 to 4 minutes, or until halfway cooked. Remove the beef from the pan and set aside. Repeat the process with the other half of the beef.

2. Add the onions and cabbage slaw to the pan and stir fry until soft, about 3 minutes. Add the stir-fry vegetables, teriyaki marinade, and red curry paste. Cook and stir until vegetables are tender and sauce has thickened a little bit, about 2 to 3 minutes. Add the beef back to the pan, stir to combine, and serve.

Tools

large sauté pan

Grocery List

Fresh

1½ pounds beef for stir-fry
1 medium red onion

Packaged

16-ounce package Mann's
Sunny Shores® California Stir
Fry®
16-ounce package Dole®
cabbage slaw
21-ounce bottle Soy Vay® Veri
Veri Teriyaki marinade
4-ounce jar Thai Kitchen®
red curry paste

Staples

cooking oil

less than 15
minutes

Beef and Snow Pea Quick Fry

To cook very quickly, your pan or wok will have to be very, very hot. Put the pan on the stove, turn the heat on high, and go watch *The Godfather*. When the movie is over, your pan will be hot enough. (Kidding, but I do mean extremely hot.) –R

Tools

medium saucepan

large sauté pan

Grocery List

Fresh

1½ pounds beef-stir-fry meat
4 cups snow peas
1 lime

Packaged

7-ounce package Minute® rice
1.75-ounce container Chinese five-spice powder
1-ounce package fresh mint

Staples

chicken broth
cooking oil
honey

1. In a medium saucepan bring 1½ cups of the chicken broth to a boil. Stir in the rice. Bring to a boil again, turn off heat, cover, and allow rice to absorb the liquid for 5 minutes.

2. Meanwhile, heat the oil in a large sauté pan or wok over high heat until very, very hot. Add the beef and season with salt and pepper. Sear the beef until golden brown, stirring occasionally, about 2 to 3 minutes. Add the snow peas and cook until translucent, about 1 minute, stirring frequently. Add Chinese five-spice powder and stir to mix in. Add the honey and the remaining ½ cup of chicken broth and bring mixture to a simmer. Season to taste with salt and pepper.

3. Fluff the rice with a fork and divide it among four plates. Scatter the mint over the top of the beef, mixing it in as you spoon an equal amount of beef over each bed of rice. Squeeze fresh lime juice over the top of each dish.

Serves 4

- 2 cups chicken broth
- 2 cups Minute® rice
- 1 tablespoon cooking oil
- 1½ pounds beef stir-fry meat
  Salt and freshly ground pepper
- 4 cups fresh snow peas
- 1 teaspoon Chinese five-spice powder
- 4 tablespoons honey
- 1 cup fresh mint leaves, roughly chopped
- 1 lime

Fried **Beef** with Broccoli and Garlic Sauce

less than 30 minutes

I don't cook fried foods that often, but every once in a while that's all that will do. Fried food is great when it's super crispy and tossed in a sweet, sticky, garlicky sauce—just like this. –R

Serves 4

1½   **pounds very thinly sliced beef for stir-fry**

3   **cups all-purpose flour**

¼   **cup cooking oil**
    Salt and freshly ground pepper

2   **teaspoons Asian-style chili-garlic sauce**

¼   **cup Amore®garlic paste or 12 garlic cloves, chopped**

1   **large head of broccoli, cut into florets, or 1 12-ounce package Dole® broccoli slaw**

1   **cup chicken broth**

½   **cup hoisin sauce**

1. Heat a large nonstick sauté pan over high heat. Dredge the beef in the flour and shake off any excess. Add half of the oil to the pan and let it get very hot. Season the beef with salt and pepper. Add half of the beef to the pan and stir-fry until browned, about 2 to 3 minutes. Remove beef from pan to a clean plate. Repeat with the other half of the beef. Drain off any excess oil.

2. Add the chili-garlic sauce, garlic, and broccoli or broccoli slaw. Stir-fry until fragrant, about 1 minute. Add chicken broth and hoisin sauce and bring mixture to a simmer. Add the beef back to the pan. Simmer for about 2 minutes to thicken the sauce slightly, then serve.

Tools

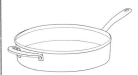

large nonstick sauté pan

Grocery List

Fresh

1½ pounds beef for stir-fry
1 large head of broccoli

Packaged

8-ounce jar Asian-style chili-garlic sauce
3.15-ounce Amore® tube garlic paste
8-ounce jar hoisin sauce

Staples

flour
cooking oil
chicken broth

Beef, Miso, and Shiitake Stir-Fry

Shiitake mushrooms have a slightly sour—almost bitter—quality that makes them just right for dishes made with miso. Miso is sweet and salty; when you add sour and bitter, you get a perfect combination of all four primary flavors. –R

Tools

large sauté pan

Grocery List

Fresh

1½ to 1¾ pounds beef stir-fry meat
7 ounces shiitake mushrooms
1 bunch scallions

Packaged

6-ounce container low-salt miso paste

Staples

extra-virgin olive oil
tomato paste
chicken broth

1. Heat a wok or large sauté pan over high heat. Add 2 tablespoons of the oil and heat until oil shimmers and starts to smoke. Season the beef with salt and pepper. Add half of the beef to the pan and brown quickly—but do not fully cook the meat—in the hot oil. Remove the beef from the pan and set aside; repeat with 2 tablespoons oil and the other half of meat.

2. Heat the pan over very high heat again. Add 1 tablespoon of the oil to the pan. Add the mushrooms and sauté them, stirring occasionally, until they are light brown, about 1 minute. Add the tomato paste and sauté for about 1 minute. Stir the miso paste into the mixture, and then the chicken broth. Add the beef to the pan and bring the stew to a quick boil for only half a minute. Sprinkle the scallions on top and serve.

Serves 4

5   tablespoons Bertolli® extra-virgin olive oil or grapeseed oil
    Salt and freshly ground pepper
1½- to 1¾-pounds beef stir-fry meat
7   ounces shiitake mushrooms, stems removed, cut in half (or cut in quarters if they're large)
2   tablespoons tomato paste
3   tablespoons low-salt miso paste
1   cup chicken broth
1   bunch scallions, cut on a diagonal

Beef and Crispy Potatoes with Blue Cheese

less than 15 minutes

This is my modern American take on a really tasty Swiss dish called *emincé de veau.* Translation: very thinly sliced veal with mushrooms and cream. It's often served on crispy potato pancakes called *rösti.* —R

Serves 4

- 4 ounces crumbled blue cheese
- ½ cup sour cream
- 3 large Idaho potatoes, peeled and grated
  Salt and freshly ground pepper
- ⅓ cup Bertolli® extra-virgin olive oil
- 1½ pounds very thinly sliced beef for stir-fry
- 1 medium red onion, sliced

See photo, page 66.

1. In a medium bowl, stir together the crumbled blue cheese and sour cream.

2. Heat a large sauté pan over medium high heat. In a large bowl, season the grated potatoes with salt and pepper. Add half of the olive oil to the pan. Divide the potato into 4 portions. Over the sink, squeeze each potato portion like a snowball to remove excess liquid. Lay the potato portions in the pan and press to form four large but very thin, lacy pancakes (about ½ inch thick and 6 inches wide—use two pans if you need to.) Cook potatoes on one side for about 2 minutes, then flip and cook on the other side for about 2 minutes more. When the potatoes are dark brown, they're done. Remove pancakes from the pan and place on four plates.

3. Add the remaining olive oil to the pan. Season the beef with salt and pepper. Stir-fry the beef and onion just until beef reaches medium doneness, about 3 to 4 minutes.

4. Top the potato pancakes with the beef and onion mixture. Dollop each with the blue cheese sauce and serve.

Tools

large sauté pan

Grocery List

Fresh

3 large Idaho potatoes
1½ pounds beef for stir-fry

Packaged

4 ounces blue cheese
8-ounce container sour cream

Staples

extra-virgin olive oil
red onion

less than 30
minutes

Beef and Mushroom Chili

I don't use allspice often, so when I do it's strategic. Allspice tastes like a combination of cinnamon, cloves, black pepper, and nutmeg, so you need to be careful how much you use and when. In this chili, it's right on. –R

Tools

large sauté pan

1. Heat a large sauté pan over high heat. When it's really hot, add the ground beef. Season the beef with salt and pepper, and cook it until the fat melts and beef browns just a little bit.

2. Add the onions and cook them with the beef until soft, stirring occasionally. Add the mushrooms and cook them until soft. Season with salt and pepper. Add the beans, tomatoes, and allspice. Bring chili to a simmer. Season to taste with salt and pepper.

3. Divide the chili among four bowls. Sprinkle the Swiss cheese on top of each bowl and serve.

Serves 4

1½ pounds 80 percent lean ground beef
    Salt and freshly ground pepper
2   cups diced onions
2   pounds mixed wild or domestic mushrooms
2   15-ounce cans Progresso® white navy beans, rinsed and drained
1   28-ounce can crushed tomatoes
2   teaspoons ground allspice
½   cup grated Swiss cheese

Grocery List

Fresh

1½ pounds 80 percent lean ground beef
2 pounds mixed wild mushrooms

Packaged

2 15-ounce cans Progresso® white navy beans
1 28-ounce can crushed tomatoes
8-ounce package Swiss cheese

Staples

onion
ground allspice

Beef and Potato Gratin

Sometimes you just want meat and potatoes—and cheese. (I actually want that combination a lot.) Yum! This ridiculously simple-to-prepare casserole goes together on the stove top in minutes and gets a cheesy crust under the broiler. —R

Serves 4

1   2-pound package Diner's Choice® Garlic Mashed Potatoes, or other mashed potatoes of choice

1   tablespoon cooking oil

1½   pounds ground beef

1   cup frozen peas

1¼   cups Campbell's® Select™ Gold Label creamy portobello mushroom soup

    Salt and freshly ground pepper

1   8-ounce package shredded sharp cheddar cheese

1. Preheat broiler on high. Microwave mashed potatoes, according to the package instructions, until hot.

2. Heat a large sauté pan over high heat until very hot. Add the oil. Add ground beef and cook, stirring, to break up meat. After about 3 minutes, add the peas and soup and bring to a simmer. Season with salt and pepper to taste.

3. Transfer beef mixture to a 9×13-inch baking dish. Spread the mashed potatoes evenly over the beef mixture, covering it completely. Sprinkle cheese evenly over the potatoes. Place under broiler until cheese melts and browns slightly, about 2 to 3 minutes. (Watch carefully so it doesn't burn.) Serve hot.

Tools

large sauté pan

9×13-inch baking dish

Grocery List

Fresh

1½ pounds ground beef

Packaged

2-pound package Diner's Choice® garlic mashed potatoes
10-ounce package frozen peas
18.3-ounce box Campbell's® Select™ Gold Label creamy portobello mushroom soup
1 8-ounce package shredded sharp cheddar cheese

Staples

cooking oil

less than 30
minutes

Ground **Beef** and Gnocchi Pie

Gnocchi pie may sound silly at first, but think about it: Gnocchi (pronounced "no-key") are made from potatoes. Combine them with ground beef, cream, and cheese, and I think shepherd's pie. Makes sense now, right? —R

Tools

stockpot

large sauté pan

Grocery List

Fresh

1½ pounds ground beef
½ pound bacon

Packaged

8-ounce carton heavy cream
8-ounce package Swiss cheese
16-ounce package Sclafani®
gnocchi

Staples

red onion
ground nutmeg

1. Heat the broiler on high.

2. In a large stockpot or Dutch oven, bring 4 quarts of water to a boil. Season water with salt and pepper and cook gnocchi according to the package instructions.

3. Meanwhile, heat a large sauté pan over high heat. Add the bacon and cook for about 3 minutes. Add the beef and onions and sauté for 5 minutes, stirring with a wooden spoon to break up the meat. When the meat is browned, add the nutmeg and cream and simmer for 3 minutes. Season mixture to taste with salt and pepper.

4. Add the cooked gnocchi to the pan and toss until the beef and gnocchi are well combined. Transfer the mixture to a large flameproof casserole and top with the cheese. Place the casserole under the broiler until the cheese is melted and golden brown.

Serves 4

Salt and freshly ground pepper
1 16-ounce package Sclafani® gnocchi (or other fresh vacuum-packed gnocchi)
½ pound bacon, diced
1½ pounds ground beef
1 medium red onion, diced
¼ teaspoon ground nutmeg
1 cup heavy cream
1 cup grated Swiss cheese

Beef and Goat Cheese Raviolos

less than 30 minutes

I once worked in the kitchen of Tom Colicchio, of the television show *Top Chef*. He used to make these open, free-form, really easy ravioli. I've been a fan of Tom and his raviolos ever since. –R

Serves 4

- 8 lasagna noodles, preferably fresh
- 7 tablespoons Bertolli® extra-virgin olive oil
- 1 medium onion, cut in small dice
- 2 teaspoons Amore® garlic paste or 3 large cloves garlic, chopped
- 1½ pounds ground beef
- 2½ tablespoons chopped fresh oregano or 1½ tablespoons dried oregano
  Salt and freshly ground pepper to taste
- 2 medium ripe tomatoes, cut into bite-size pieces
- 1 11-ounce log goat cheese
- 2 tablespoons red wine vinegar

See photo, page 67.

1. Cook lasagna noodles according to package directions.

2. Meanwhile, heat 4 tablespoons of the olive oil in a very large sauté pan over medium heat. Add the onion and sauté, stirring often, for about 2 minutes. Add the garlic and sauté 1 minute more. Add the beef, stirring to break into small chunks. (If using dried oregano, add 1 tablespoon at this stage.)

3. Season meat with salt and pepper and cook until the beef is just cooked through. Gently toss in the tomatoes and cheese (if using fresh oregano add 2 tablespoons here), and cook until mixture is hot throughout, about 2 minutes.

4. In a small bowl, whisk vinegar with remaining olive oil and remaining fresh or dried oregano, and season to taste with salt and pepper.

5. Lay down one lasagna noodle on each plate and divide the beef mixture over the noodles. Top off each plate with one more noodle.

6. Drizzle the vinaigrette over the raviolos and serve.

Tools

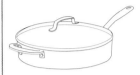

large sauté pan

Grocery List

Fresh

12-ounce package lasagna noodles
1½ pounds ground beef
2 medium tomatoes

Packaged

3.15-ounce Amore® tube garlic paste
1-ounce package fresh oregano
11-ounce package goat cheese

Staples

extra-virgin olive oil
onion
red wine vinegar

Sautéed **Beef** with Spicy Sweet Potato Fries

When it comes to tender cuts of beef, there are lots of choices, including strip steak, ribeye, and filet mignon. But if you want to spend less money, try cube steak (as I used here), sirloin tips, flat-iron steak, or beef round—just don't overcook it. –R

Tools

large sauté pan

Grocery List

Fresh

2 pounds beef tips
1 cup cherry tomatoes
1 bunch cilantro

Packaged

15-ounce package Alexia®
frozen julienne sweet potato
fries
25-ounce jar Victoria® Fra
Diavolo pasta sauce

Staples

crushed red pepper flakes
extra-virgin olive oil
curry powder

1. Preheat oven to 375°F. Cook the sweet potato fries according to the package instructions for baking. When they're done, toss them in a bowl with the crushed red pepper flakes and salt and pepper.

2. Heat a large sauté pan over high heat. Pour the olive oil into the pan and let it get extremely hot, to the point it begins to smoke. Pat the beef dry with a clean paper towel. Season the beef with salt and pepper. Carefully place the beef into the hot pan and brown it quickly without overcooking, stirring occasionally, about 2 to 3 minutes.

3. Add the cherry tomatoes to the pan and allow them to get just warmed through. Stir in the curry powder and the Fra Diavolo pasta sauce. Bring the mixture to a slow simmer. Stir in the cilantro. Season with salt and pepper to taste and serve.

Serves 4

1 **15-ounce package Alexia®
   frozen julienne sweet
   potato fries**
½ **teaspoon crushed red
   pepper flakes**
**Salt and freshly ground
   pepper**
2 **tablespoons Bertolli™
   extra-virgin olive oil or
   grapeseed oil**
2 **pounds beef tips (or your
   favorite tender cut of
   beef), cut into small
   squares**
1 **cup cherry tomatoes**
1 **tablespoon curry powder**
½ **cup Victoria® Fra Diavolo
   sauce**
½ **cup fresh cilantro, rough
   chopped**

See photo, page 77.

Beef Pot Roast with Cauliflower and Gravy

less than 30 minutes

Classic pot roast takes an hour or two to prepare—not 15 or 20 minutes. But as with many of the dishes in the book, I've transformed a time-consuming and labor-intensive dish into a flavorful gem that won't take over your schedule. —R

Serves 4

- 4 tablespoons cooking oil
- 2 pounds sirloin tips
  Salt and freshly ground pepper
- 1 large onion, cut in large dice
- ½ teaspoon Amore® garlic paste, or 1 small garlic clove, chopped
- ½ cup red wine
- 3 12-ounce jars Heinz® pork gravy
- 1 head cauliflower, cut into very small florets

1. In a Dutch oven, heat 2 tablespoons of the oil over very high heat. Pat the beef dry with a clean paper towel and season generously with salt and pepper. Cook half of the beef in the hot oil, stirring occasionally to make sure all sides are browned, about 2 to 3 minutes. Transfer browned beef to a clean plate and repeat with the remaining oil and the other half of the beef.

2. Turn the heat down to medium. Add the onion and sauté until almost tender, about 3 minutes. Add garlic and continue to cook for 1 minute more. Add wine to the pan and reduce by half. Add the gravy and bring to a simmer.

3. Return beef to the Dutch oven. Add the cauliflower and simmer until the cauliflower is tender. Season with salt and pepper to taste and serve meat with gravy and vegetables.

Tools

Dutch oven

Grocery List

Fresh

2 pounds sirloin tips
1 head cauliflower

Packaged

3.15-ounce Amore® tube garlic paste
3 12-ounce jars Heinz® pork gravy

Staples

cooking oil
onion
red wine

less than 30 minutes

Roast Beef with Figs and Black Pepper

My grandmother had four fig trees on her Long Island farm. As a kid I used to collect them by hand—so no fig will ever beat that for me. But dried figs are very good. They retain the rich, sweet fig flavor, and if they're rehydrated it's almost like using fresh. —R

Tools

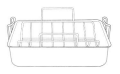

blender

roasting pan

Grocery List

Fresh

2½ pounds center-cut beef tenderloin

Packaged

2 9-ounce packages
Sun-Maid® dried Mission figs

Staples

honey
red wine vinegar
ground cinnamon

1. Preheat the oven to 375°F.

2. Strain the figs, reserving the water. Save a third of the fig water, plus 1 additional measured cup of the fig water.

3. In a blender, combine a third of the soaked figs with the reserved fig water and the honey, vinegar, cracked black pepper, and cinnamon. Blend until mostly smooth, leaving a few small fig pieces remaining. Set aside.

4. Season the beef on all sides with salt and pepper. Heat a flameproof roasting pan over medium-high on the stove top and add the oil. Brown the roast on all sides in the roasting pan; transfer the pan to the oven. Roast for 10 minutes, then remove from oven and spread the fig puree over the top of the tenderloin. Add the remaining figs and the 1 cup fig water to the roasting pan. Return the pan to the oven and roast for 10 minutes more. Remove from the oven and let the roast rest for 5 minutes.

5. Slice the roast and serve with the roasted figs and pan juices.

Serves 4

2	9-ounce bags Sun-Maid® dried Mission figs, soaked in enough water to cover for about 5 minutes
¼	cup honey
⅓	cup red wine vinegar
2	tablespoons cracked black pepper
1	teaspoon ground cinnamon
2½	pounds center-cut beef tenderloin
	Salt and freshly ground pepper
2	tablespoons cooking oil

POULTRY

"It's flavor first, second, and third. An average-looking but delicious dish will do the job."

less than 30
minutes

Chicken Cutlets
with Goat Cheese-Scalloped Potatoes

Great flavor comes out of a balance of tastes. The flavor hook of this dish is the combination of rich, slightly sour goat cheese combined with the acidity of lemon juice, the sweetness of pineapple, and the piney aroma of rosemary. Still not convinced? Try it. –R

Tools

9×13-inch baking dish

large sauté pan

Grocery List

Fresh

2 pounds chicken cutlets
1 bunch flat-leaf parsley

Packaged

2 15-ounce cans Libby's®
  sliced potatoes
8-ounce carton heavy cream
11-ounce log goat cheese
12-ounce jar pineapple
  preserves
1-ounce package fresh
  rosemary

Staples

butter
lemons

1. Preheat the broiler on high.

2. Arrange the potato slices in a 9×13-inch microwaveable baking dish.

3. In a small bowl, gradually mix the cream into about 4 ounces of the goat cheese. Pour this mixture evenly over the potatoes. Season the potatoes with salt and pepper. Dot the potatoes with the remaining goat cheese and microwave for 7 minutes. Remove potatoes from microwave and place under the broiler just until the potatoes begin to brown.

4. Meanwhile, heat the butter in a very large sauté pan over medium heat. Season the chicken with salt and pepper and add to the pan. Cook for about 3 minutes per side.

5. While the chicken is cooking, mix together the preserves, lemon juice, and rosemary. When the chicken is just cooked through, brush on the pineapple glaze.

6. Sprinkle the potatoes with parsley and serve with the chicken.

✱ If you can't buy chicken cutlets, you can make your own. See page 11 for directions.

Serves 4

2   15-ounce cans Libby's®
    sliced potatoes, drained
1   cup heavy cream
1   11-ounce log goat cheese
    Salt and freshly ground
    pepper
3   tablespoons butter
2   pounds chicken cutlets*
½   cup pineapple preserves
¼   cup fresh lemon juice
2   tablespoons chopped
    fresh rosemary
¼   cup chopped fresh flat-
    leaf parsley

Chicken and Wild Mushroom Marsala

less than 15 minutes

This dish is named after a city in Sicily and its famous wine, called Marsala. The intense flavor and powerful aromatics of Marsala make it hard to replace. Any wine will taste good in this dish, but if you want the real deal, seek it out—it's widely available. –R

Serves 4

- 3 tablespoons Bertolli® extra-virgin olive oil
- 12 ounces mixed wild mushrooms, stems trimmed
- 1 cup plus 1 teaspoon all-purpose flour
  Salt and freshly ground pepper
- 1½ pounds chicken cutlets*
- 12 tablespoons butter (1½ sticks)
- 1 cup Marsala wine
- 1 cup chicken broth
- 1 lemon
- ¼ cup chopped fresh flat-leaf parsley

1. Heat a large sauté pan over medium-high heat. Add the olive oil and the mushrooms and sauté until light brown, stirring occasionally, about 1 or 2 minutes. Remove mushrooms from the pan.

2. In a shallow dish, combine the 1 cup flour, salt, and pepper. Season the chicken with salt and pepper and toss in the flour mixture, coating all sides. Shake off the excess flour.

3. Melt 4 tablespoons of the butter in the sauté pan over medium-low heat. Place the chicken in the pan and cook for about 1½ to 2 minutes per side, or until just cooked through. Remove chicken from pan and keep it warm.

4. Sprinkle the teaspoon of flour in the pan and stir until it's absorbed by the butter. Stir in the Marsala and chicken broth and simmer until slightly thickened, stirring occasionally, about 2 to 3 minutes. Add the mushrooms to the pan and squeeze the juice of the lemon directly into the mushroom sauce. Add the remaining 1 stick of butter, stirring constantly to make a smooth, silky sauce.

5. Season the sauce to taste with salt and pepper and pour over the chicken. Sprinkle with chopped parsley and serve.

✱ If you can't buy chicken cutlets, you can make your own. See page 11 for directions.

Tools

large sauté pan

Grocery List

Fresh

12 ounces mixed wild mushrooms
1 bunch flat-leaf parsley

Packaged

750 ml bottle Marsala wine
1½ pounds chicken cutlets

Staples

extra-virgin olive oil
butter/flour
chicken broth/lemon

less than 30
minutes

Chicken & Cauliflower Under a Brick

If you don't eat the skin of cooked chicken because you're trying to be virtuous, give it up. Weighting skin-on chicken with a brick (*sotto mattone* in Italian) maximizes the surface area of the skin and makes it extra crispy (and so worth the indiscretion). –R

Tools

stockpot

cast-iron skillet

Grocery List

Fresh

4 boneless chicken breasts, with skin
1 head cauliflower

Packaged

1-ounce package fresh rosemary
10-ounce jar Mustapha's™ Moroccan harissa

Staples

extra-virgin olive oil

1. Preheat oven to 450°F.

2. Wrap 2 bricks in heavy-duty aluminum foil. If you don't have bricks, use a small stockpot filled with about 3 pints of room-temperature water. (Make sure that the water only reaches about halfway up the side of the pot, just in case it tips over.) Cover the bottom of the pot with foil.

3. Heat a large cast-iron skillet over high heat and add the olive oil. Season the chicken with salt and pepper and place it in the skillet, skin side down. Place one sprig of rosemary on top of each chicken breast, followed by 1 tablespoon of the harissa, then the cauliflower, divided evenly among the breasts. Place the bricks on top of the chicken and cauliflower. The chicken should flatten out.

4. The skin will brown quickly, in about 4 to 5 minutes. Lower the heat to medium-low and cook for about 4 minutes more. Carefully turn the chicken over (If it sticks, don't pull it. Let it continue cooking—it will release when the skin is crispy.) The chicken should still be tender to the touch (cooked about halfway), very crispy, and dark golden brown.

5. After flipping the chicken, transfer the skillet to the oven and cook until the cauliflower and chicken are cooked through, about 5 minutes.

Serves 4

2 tablespoons Bertolli® extra-virgin olive oil
4 boneless chicken breasts, with skin
   Salt and freshly ground pepper
4 sprigs rosemary
4 tablespoons Mustapha's™ Moroccan harissa or Thai Kitchen® curry paste
3 cups of small cauliflower florets

Grilled **Stuffed Chicken**
with Prosciutto and Peppers

less than **15**
minutes

Prosciutto is cured ham. Unlike bacon it isn't smoked, but it's never been cooked. There's some debate about whether you should ever cook prosciutto. I disregard most rules of cooking and just taste. If it tastes good, it is good—no matter what the rules say. —R

Serves 4

- 8 **4-ounce chicken cutlets (choose very thin ones)*** **Salt and freshly ground pepper**
- 8 **teaspoons (or a 4-ounce jar) pimiento slices**
- 8 **thin slices deli provolone, about ¾ ounce each, cut in half**
- 8 **slices prosciutto**
- 8 **large basil leaves**
- 4 **teaspoons Amore® garlic paste or 4 garlic cloves, chopped**
- 4 **tablespoons Bertolli® extra-virgin olive oil**

1. Preheat grill/grill pan/broiler on very high heat. Lay the chicken down on a clean work surface. Season with salt and pepper.

2. On the bottom half of each cutlet, lay down 1 teaspoon of pimiento, then a half slice of cheese. Top cheese with 1 slice of prosciutto and a basil leaf. Last, lay down remaining half slice of cheese and fold the top half of the cutlet over to cover.

3. Press down on each "package" firmly. Insert a toothpick into the end of the cutlet to help it remain closed during cooking.

4. Combine garlic and olive oil and thoroughly rub the stuffed chicken packages with this mixture. Generously season the chicken with salt and pepper and place on the grill. Grill the chicken for about 3 minutes per side, or until chicken is cooked through and cheese melts. Serve immediately.

✱ If you can't buy chicken cutlets, you can make your own. See page 11 for directions.

Tools

grill pan

Grocery List

Fresh

8 4-ounce chicken cutlets

Packaged

4-ounce jar pimientos
8-ounce package sliced provolone
2-ounce package prosciutto
1-ounce package fresh basil
3.15-ounce tube Amore® garlic paste

Staples

extra-virgin olive oil

Marinated **Fried Chicken** with Herbs

Herb Thyme® poultry bouquet is one of several prepared spice mixes that are great in that old-school way. It's hard to know what to buy if you don't have experience with premade spice mixes. Try a few in different dishes until you find a match you like. –R

Tools

large stockpot

Grocery List

Fresh

3½-pound whole chicken

Packaged

750 ml bottle Martini & Rossi® rosso vermouth
0.33-ounce package Herb Thyme® poultry bouquet

Staples

lemons
canola oil
flour/eggs

1. Place chicken in a very large heavy-duty plastic bag and pour the vermouth and lemon juice into the bag to cover the chicken. Press to release as much air as possible and seal the bag. Marinate chicken in the refrigerator for about 3 hours.

2. In a large stock pot, heat the oil to 400°F. In a shallow dish, mix together the flour, pepper, and herb mix. Remove chicken from the bag and pat dry. Dip the chicken in the eggs, turning to coat. Next, dredge the chicken in the seasoned flour.

3. Add chicken to the oil. Fry the chicken until it is cooked through, about 15 minutes for breasts and 10 minutes for legs and thighs. (The oil temperature will drop dramatically when the chicken is added to the pot—maintain it at about 300°F for the duration of the cooking time. Watch the oil temperature so that the chicken doesn't burn.) When chicken is cooked through, remove it from the oil, drain it on a paper towel-lined platter or baking sheet, and season generously with salt.

Serves 4

1 whole chicken, cut up into 8 pieces (about 3½ pounds)
1 cup Martini & Rossi® rosso vermouth
⅓ cup fresh lemon juice
¾ gallon canola oil
1½ cups flour
2 tablespoons freshly ground pepper
1 0.33-ounce package Herb Thyme® poultry bouquet or 2 teaspoons poultry seasoning
3 eggs, well beaten
Salt

Grilled **Chicken Breast**
with Lemon, Pea, and Mint Potatoes

less than 30 minutes

When I first discovered that mint and peas were a match made in heaven, I dismissed it because I was after much more groundbreaking inventions. Now that I cook at home every day, it's become my go-to garnish—or in this case, sauce. —R

Serves 4

2 tablespoons Bertolli® extra-virgin olive oil, plus more for drizzling
2 garlic cloves, chopped
4 chicken cutlets, about 5 ounces each*
 Salt and freshly ground pepper
1 cup frozen peas
½ cup fresh mint, roughly chopped
2 1-pound packages Diner's Choice® country-style mashed potatoes, or potato salad
¼ cup roughly chopped fresh basil
 Zest of 2 lemons

1. Preheat a grill to high.

2. Mix 2 tablespoons of olive oil with the garlic and slather it on the chicken. Season generously with salt and pepper. Allow chicken to marinate while preparing the peas.

3. Bring a small pot of lightly salted water to a boil. Drop in the peas and mint. Boil gently for about 4 minutes. Drain, reserving ½ cup of the cooking liquid.

4. In a small blender, puree the peas and mint with the reserved cooking liquid until smooth; set puree aside.

5. Place the chicken on the grill and cook for 3 to 4 minutes per side.

6. Meanwhile, place the potatoes in a medium saucepan and warm them through. Add the pea puree, basil, and lemon zest and mix thoroughly to combine. Season to taste with salt and pepper.

7. Drizzle the potatoes generously with olive oil and serve with the chicken.

✱ If you can't buy chicken cutlets, you can make your own. See page 11 for directions.

Tools

blender

medium saucepan

Grocery List

Fresh

4 5-ounce chicken cutlets

Packaged

10-ounce package frozen peas
1-ounce package fresh mint
2 1-pound packages Diner's Choice® country-style mashed potatoes or potato salad
1-ounce package fresh basil

Staples

extra-virgin olive oil
garlic
lemons

less than 30
minutes

Grilled **Chicken** with Avocado Relish

Buttery avocado is a good match for almost anything because of its mild flavor and creamy texture. This relish makes a good side dish for chicken, steak, fish, and shellfish. –R

Tools

grill pan

Grocery
List

Fresh

8 chicken cutlets
3 large avocados
1 jalapeño pepper
1 bunch cilantro

Packaged

Staples

extra-virgin olive oil
red onion/tomato
lime

1. Preheat a grill/grill pan/broiler on high.

2. Coat the chicken with 2 tablespoons of the olive oil and season generously with salt and pepper. Grill the chicken until it is cooked throughout, about 3½ minutes per side (total time depends on thickness).

3. While the chicken is grilling, make the relish.

4. In a medium-size bowl, combine the avocado, tomato, onion, jalapeño, lime juice, and remaining olive oil. Season to taste with salt and pepper. Gently fold in cilantro.

5. Slice chicken and serve alongside a mound of the relish.

✱ If you can't buy chicken cutlets, you can make your own. See page 11 for directions.

tip You can make the relish ahead and chill it. Just make sure it's covered with paper towels soaked in lemon juice touching the surface of it so the avocado doesn't start to turn brown.

Serves 4
8   chicken cutlets*
3   tablespoons Bertolli®
     extra-virgin olive oil
     Salt and freshly ground
     pepper
3   large avocados, diced
1   large tomato, diced
1   medium red onion, diced
1   jalapeño, finely chopped
     Juice of 1 lime
½   cup fresh cilantro, roughly
     chopped

Chicken Kabobs in Hoisin with Grilled Corn

There are lots of good things about grilling corn. It's faster than boiling, and you get a more flavorful end result, with some great-tasting charred bits.* When you mix the jam with the hoisin, use my amounts as a guide but create a blend that's good to you. —R

Serves 4

¾ cup (or 7.25 oz jar) hoisin sauce
⅔ cup apricot jam
Juice of 1 lemon
4 prepared chicken kabobs
4 ears of corn, shucked
Bertolli® extra-virgin olive oil, for brushing
Salt and freshly ground pepper
Butter

1. Heat a grill/grill pan/broiler on high.

2. Mix together the hoisin, jam, and lemon juice; reserve ⅓ of the mixture. Toss the kabobs with the remaining mixture and let marinate while you cook the corn.

3. Brush corn with olive oil and season generously with salt and pepper. Place the corn on the grilling surface. Grill, turning often, for about 15 minutes, or until it is beautifully charred and the kernels are tender.

4. When the corn has been cooking for about 5 minutes, remove the kabobs from the marinade and season generously with salt and pepper. Place on the grill and cook, turning occasionally, for about 9 minutes, or until chicken is just cooked through.

5. Remove kabobs from the grill and brush with the reserved marinade.

6. Serve kabobs with the grilled corn, with butter for spreading on the kernels.

✱ If you don't want the corn to char, grill it in the husk. The effect is the same as boiling because you are essentially steaming it—and you don't have to worry about a pot on the stove while you are outside grilling.

Tools

grill pan

Grocery List

Fresh

4 prepared chicken kabobs
4 ears of corn, shucked

Packaged

7.25 ounce jar hoisin sauce
12-ounce jar apricot jam

Staples

lemon
extra-virgin olive oil
butter

Chicken Breast
with Fresh Fig and Arugula Salad

I can't say enough about fruit as a flavor detonator—especially when it's combined with herbs and spices. Fruit and herbs may seem like an odd combination, but think of it this way: Basil is an anise-flavored herb. Think licorice. Makes sense now, doesn't it? —R

Tools

large sauté pan

Grocery List

Fresh

4 boneless chicken breasts with skin
8 fresh figs
10 ounces arugula

Packaged

1-ounce package fresh basil

Staples

extra-virgin olive oil
red wine vinegar
red wine/honey

1. Preheat oven to 350°F.

2. Heat a large, ovenproof sauté pan over high heat. Pour in the 2 tablespoons olive oil. Season the chicken breasts with salt and pepper. Place the chicken, skin side down, in the hot pan and put the pan in the oven. Cook for 10 minutes.

3. Meanwhile, in a large bowl mix the vinegar, wine, honey, remaining oil, basil, and fruit.

4. Turn the chicken breasts over and let cook for an additional 5 minutes.

5. Toss the arugula with fig mixture and season to taste with salt and pepper.

6. Place a chicken breast on each of four plates and pile the fig and arugula salad on top.

Serves 4

½   cup plus 2 tablespoons Bertolli® extra-virgin olive oil
4   boneless chicken breasts, with skin
     Salt and freshly ground pepper
¼   cup red wine vinegar
¼   cup red wine
¼   teaspoon honey
½   cup fresh basil, torn
8   fresh figs (or small sickle pears) cut in half
10 ounces arugula

See photo, page 79.

Chicken Scaloppine in an Artichoke Broth

less than 30 minutes

In the 1990s the word "nage" was ubiquitous on the menus of all the great restaurants in New York. It means "swim" in French. The idea was to float something—usually fish—in a pool of very light broth. It delivers great flavor in a low-fat, low-carb dish. –R

Serves 4

- 2   16-ounce packages Alexia® frozen mashed potatoes, any style you prefer
- 2   tablespoons cooking oil
- 8   3- to 4-ounce chicken cutlets*
  Salt and freshly ground pepper
- 3   tablespoons Bertolli® extra-virgin olive oil
- 1   tablespoon Amore® garlic paste, or 3 garlic cloves, chopped
- 2   tablespoons fresh thyme
- 2   14-ounce cans quartered artichoke hearts, with liquid

See photo, page 78.

1. Heat the mashed potatoes according to the package instructions.

2. Heat a very large sauté pan over medium-low heat. Add the oil and let it get hot. Season the chicken lightly with salt and pepper. Place half of the chicken in the pan and cook for about 2 minutes per side. Remove from the pan and repeat with the other half of the chicken. Set chicken aside near the stove top to keep it warm.

3. Add the olive oil to the pan and turn the heat up to medium. Sauté the garlic and thyme in the olive oil until fragrant but not brown. Add the artichokes and artichoke liquid and bring to a boil. Simmer until artichoke hearts are hot throughout. Season to taste with salt and pepper.

4. To serve, place a mound of the potatoes in the center of each serving plate. Top each mound with 2 chicken cutlets. Spoon the artichokes and broth over the top and serve.

✳ If you can't buy chicken cutlets, you can make your own. See page 11 for directions.

Tools

very large sauté pan

Grocery List

Fresh

8 3- to 4-ounce chicken cutlets

Packaged

2 16-ounce packages Alexia® frozen mashed potatoes
3.15-ounce tube Amore® garlic paste
1-ounce package fresh thyme
2 14-ounce cans quartered artichoke hearts

Staples

cooking oil
extra-virgin olive oil

less than 30 minutes

Chicken Scaloppine
with Potato Pancakes and Port Sauce

All wines are some combination of sweet, sour, and bitter flavors. Port, a dessert wine, is very sweet. A little vinegar helps balance the overall flavor of the sauce, but it's still sweet. I really like the sweetness over the chicken and potato pancakes. —R

Tools

2 large sauté pans

Grocery List

Fresh

1½ pounds chicken cutlets
1 bunch chives

Packaged

10.5-ounce package Dr. Praeger's® frozen potato pancakes
750-ml bottle red port wine

Staples

butter/flour
red wine vinegar
extra-virgin olive oil

1. In a large sauté pan, melt 4 tablespoons of the butter over medium heat.

2. In a shallow dish, season the flour with salt and pepper. Sprinkle the chicken lightly with salt and pepper and toss it in the flour. Add chicken to the pan and cook about 2 minutes per side, or just until cooked through. Remove the chicken from pan and cover lightly with aluminum foil to keep warm.

3. Add the port and vinegar to the pan and bring to a simmer; reduce by half. Add the remaining 4 tablespoons of the butter and cook, stirring, until it's slightly reduced to a sauce consistency. Season with salt and lots of pepper.

4. In a separate large sauté pan, heat the oil over medium heat. Add the potato pancakes and fry until golden brown, about 3½ minutes per side. Place on a paper towel-lined plate and season with salt and pepper.

5. Add chicken back to the pan with the sauce in it. Sprinkle the chives on top and serve chicken with port sauce and potato pancakes.

✳ If you can't buy chicken cutlets, you can make your own. See page 11 for directions.

Serves 4

- 8 tablespoons butter (1 stick)
- 1 cup all-purpose flour
  Salt and freshly ground pepper
- 1¼ pounds chicken cutlets*
- ½ cup red port wine
- 1 tablespoon red wine vinegar
- ½ cup Bertolli® extra-virgin olive oil
- 4 frozen Dr. Praeger's® potato pancakes or latkes
- 2 tablespoons chopped fresh chives

Molten **Chicken Cutlets** with Kale

less than 15 minutes

I love to use thin chicken cutlets because they cook very fast. Chicken breast is almost 100 percent lean so it tends to be dry even if cooked perfectly. So I decided to put some cheese between the cutlets. Anything made with cheese and fried tastes great. –R

Serves 4

½ cup cooking oil
8 4-ounce thin chicken cutlets*
   Salt and freshly ground pepper
8 ounces sliced Gruyère, Swiss, or provolone cheese
1 cup corn tortilla flour (also called masa harina)
2 eggs, beaten until frothy
3 tablespoons Bertolli® extra-virgin olive oil
4 cups of Cut 'n Clean Greens™ kale, or 2 bunches fresh kale, washed well and chopped

1. Heat 2 large sauté pans over medium heat. Pour the cooking oil into one of the pans.

2. Meanwhile, season chicken breasts with salt and pepper. Firmly press 2 ounces of the sliced cheese onto each of the 4 chicken breasts. Place the other 4 breasts on top and press firmly.

3. Place the corn flour and eggs in separate shallow dishes. Dredge the chicken-cheese stacks in the flour and then dip into the eggs, turning to coat. Finally, dredge each stack thoroughly in the corn flour again.

4. Place chicken in pan with cooking oil and sauté until golden brown, about 3 minutes per side. The cheese should be melted.

5. While the chicken is cooking, add the olive oil and kale to the other sauté pan. Season to taste with salt and pepper. Cook over high heat until tender, stirring occasionally, about 4 minutes.

6. When chicken is cooked through, serve it on top of a pile of the hot kale.

✱ If you can't buy chicken cutlets, you can make your own. See page 11 for directions.

Tools

2 large sauté pans

Grocery List

Fresh

8 4-ounce chicken cutlets
2 1-pound packages Cut 'n Clean Greens™ kale

Packaged

8-ounce package sliced Gruyére, Swiss or provolone cheese
2-pound package corn tortilla flour

Staples

cooking oil
eggs
extra-virgin olive oil

Pan-Fried **Swiss Chicken** Bundles

less than 15
minutes

I love escarole—and for good reason. It's a great source of vitamins A and C. It cooks quickly—one of the few greens from the chicory family that does—and it's less bitter than its cousins. You can also eat it cooked or in salad form, as it is here. –R

Tools

2 large sauté pans

Grocery List

Fresh

8 4-ounce chicken cutlets

Packaged

8-ounce package sliced Swiss cheese
2-pound package corn tortilla flour
10-ounce package Dole® Italian salad blend

Staples

cooking oil
eggs/sherry vinegar
extra-virgin olive oil

1. Heat two large sauté pans over medium heat. Put ½ cup oil in each and allow it to get hot.

2. Lay the chicken cutlets on a work surface and season with salt and pepper. Lay down 1 slice of the cheese across the top of each cutlet to cover the entire surface. Press the cheese evenly and firmly onto the cutlets. Roll the cutlets and cheese into a pinwheel. Season with salt and pepper again. Secure by pushing 2 toothpicks through the rolls, top to bottom.

3. Put the corn flour in a shallow dish and dredge the rolls in it. Dip each roll into the beaten eggs and then again into the corn flour, turning to coat evenly. When the oil is hot, place two rolls in each pan. Cook for a total of about 8 minutes, about 2 minutes on each of the four "sides" of the chicken.

4. Chicken should be golden brown and crispy. Check doneness by putting the tip of a knife, a skewer, or a fork into the center of each roll and then touching it to see if it's hot.

5. While the chicken is cooking, combine the sherry vinegar with the olive oil and toss with the escarole. Season the salad to taste with salt and pepper and serve a small pile along with each chicken roll.

✱ If you can't buy chicken cutlets, you can make your own. See page 11 for directions.

Serves 4

1	cup cooking oil
8	chicken cutlets (about 4 ounces each)*
	Salt and freshly ground pepper
8	slices Swiss cheese
	Toothpicks
1	cup corn tortilla flour (also called masa harina)
3	eggs, well beaten
1	tablespoon plus 2 teaspoons sherry vinegar
2	tablespoons Bertolli® extra-virgin olive oil
1	10-ounce bag Dole® Italian salad blend

Pan-Roasted **Chicken Breast**
with Pickled Peppers

I'm a big fan of peppers. My grandmother used to preserve many varieties, so I think of myself as a bit of a pepper aficionado. The quality of store-bought pepper preserves is superb. They're a good example of a shortcut food that saves time and tastes great. —R

less than 30 minutes

Serves 4

- ¼ cup Bertolli® extra-virgin olive oil
- 4 boneless chicken breasts, with skin
  Salt and freshly ground pepper
- ⅛ cup honey
- 1 cup pear nectar
- ¼ cup red wine vinegar
- 1 12-ounce jar Mancini® red pimiento peppers, drained
- 1 12-ounce jar Mancini® fried peppers
- 1 10-ounce box frozen okra, thawed

1. Heat a large skillet over high heat. When it's hot, add the olive oil. Heat the olive oil until it shimmers and it is almost smoking. Season the skin side of chicken breasts with salt and pepper. Carefully place the chicken skin side down into the pan. Cook until skin is brown and crispy, about 8 minutes. Season the top of the chicken with salt and pepper and turn it over. Continue cooking until it's done, about 3 minutes.

2. Meanwhile, combine honey and pear nectar in a large saucepan over high heat. Cook, stirring occasionally, until it's reduced and very thick, about 5 minutes. Add the vinegar, pimientos, and fried peppers. Bring mixture to a simmer. Add the okra and simmer for 3 minutes. Season with salt and pepper to taste.

3. Spoon pepper mixture on top of chicken (skin side up) and serve.

Tools

large skillet

large saucepan

Grocery List

Fresh

4 boneless chicken breasts

Packaged

12-ounce can pear nectar
12-ounce jar Mancini® red pimiento peppers
12-ounce jar Mancini® fried peppers
10-ounce box frozen okra

Staples

extra-virgin olive oil
honey
red wine vinegar

Pork Medallions with Apricot and Endive, page 116

Beef and Crispy Potatoes with Blue Cheese, page 40 (above) ; Beef and Goat Cheese Raviolos, page 44 (opposite page);
Chicken Breasts with Cauliflower and Citrus, page 83 (opposite page)

Grilled Pork Chops and Peppers alla Brace page 104
(above left); Horseradish-and-Cinnamon-Marinated
Skirt Steak with Pears and Scallions page 23 (above right
and opposite page)

Flank Steak Forestière, page 25 (above); Boiled Beef and Pappardelle, page 32 (opposite page)

Fried Pork Cutlets with Chopped Salad, page 102 (above);

Perfect Roasted Chicken Smothered in Caramelized Onions, page 214 (opposite page, upper right)

Chicken with Turmeric & Onions, page 85 (opposite page, lower left)

Open-Faced Lamb Sandwich with Cucumber Raita, page 130 (above);
Cinnamon-Rubbed Grilled Lamb Chops with Sweet Potatoes, page 131 (opposite page)

Pork Burgers with Walnuts and Chow Chow, page 112

Pork Chops Puttanesca, page 106 (lower left)
Sautéed Beef with Spicy Sweet Potato Fries, page 45 (lower right)

Chicken Scaloppine in an Artichoke Broth, page 60 (above);
Chicken Breast with Fresh Fig and Arugula Salad, page 59 (opposite page)

Meatloaf with Fried Onions and Tomato Gravy, page 210

less than 30 minutes

Stuffed Chicken Breasts
with Giant White Beans

One of my go-to condiments is mustard. It's sour, salty, bitter, and spicy. If you add something sweet, like mayonnaise or ketchup, you've got a real winner of a sauce. Now Hellmann's® makes Dijonnaise, so the work is all done for you. —R

Tools

2 large sauté pans

large saucepan

Grocery List

Fresh

8 chicken cutlets
(1¼ pound total)

Packaged

8-ounce package mozzarella
2 14-ounce cans white gigante beans
10.75-ounce bottle Hellman's® Dijonnaise™
1-ounce package fresh basil

Staples

cooking oil
flour/breadcrumbs
eggs

1. Heat 2 large sauté pans over medium heat. Add half of the cooking oil to each pan and allow to get hot.

2. Place the flour, eggs, and breadcrumbs in three separate large shallow dishes. On a work surface, lay out 4 chicken cutlets. Place a slice of mozzarella in the middle of the chicken cutlet. Top each with another chicken cutlet and press firmly. Season with salt and pepper.

3. With your left hand, dredge each chicken stack in the flour, brushing off excess with your right hand. Then dip each stack into the beaten eggs. With your left hand, again dredge the stacks in the breadcrumbs. Use your dry hand to press the crumbs into the chicken. Gently shake off any excess.

4. Place 2 cutlet stacks into each pan. They should sizzle immediately and begin to brown. Cook for about 3 minutes, then carefully turn the chicken and cook for another 3 minutes, until cooked through. Remove from pan and drain on a paper towel-lined platter.

5. Meanwhile, in a large saucepan heat the beans with the reserved ¼ cup of liquid until warm. Add the Dijonnaise and the basil, stirring to combine. Serve each stuffed chicken cutlet with a side of seasoned beans.

✳ If you can't buy chicken cutlets, you can make your own. See page 11 for directions.

Serves 4

½ cup cooking oil
2 cups all-purpose flour
3 eggs, well beaten
1½ cups breadcrumbs
8 chicken cutlets (just under 1¼ pounds total)*
½ pound mozzarella, sliced
Salt and freshly ground black pepper
2 14-ounce cans white "gigante" beans, drained, ¼ cup of liquid reserved
4 tablespoons Hellmann's® Dijonnaise™
3 tablespoons roughly chopped fresh basil

Puffy Chicken with White Beans & Curry

It's called "puffy" because the noodles puff up when you fry them. But I have to admit that "Diddy," formerly known as "Puff Daddy" and then "Puffy," was a guest at my restaurant, Union Pacific. I made a version of this for him. He thought it was hilarious. –R

Serves 4

1   9-ounce package thin rice noodles
8   3- to 4-ounce chicken cutlets*
1   egg white, slightly beaten
     Cooking oil
     Salt and freshly ground pepper
2   15-ounce cans Progresso® cannellini beans
4   tablespoons red curry paste
1   cup basil leaves, torn

See photo, page 178.

1. With good-quality, clean kitchen shears, cut the rice noodles into ½-inch pieces.

2. Coat one side of the chicken cutlets with the egg white, then coat with the rice noodles, pressing the noodles into the chicken to make them stick.

3. In a large sauté pan, add 1 inch of cooking oil. Heat the oil over medium-high until it's hot enough so that when a rice noodle is dropped in, it instantly puffs up. Gently place 2 pieces of the chicken in the pan. Fry for about 30 seconds, then carefully flip the chicken. Fry for another 30 seconds, until noodles are puffy and crisp and chicken is cooked through. Drain on a paper towel-lined platter and season to taste with salt and pepper. Repeat with remaining chicken.

4. While chicken is cooking, heat the white beans with the curry paste in a small saucepan. When hot, add basil. Serve puffy chicken cutlet on top of beans.

✱ If you can't buy chicken cutlets, you can make your own. See page 11 for directions.

Tools

large sauté pan

small saucepan

Grocery List

Fresh

8 3- to 4-ounce chicken cutlets

Packaged

1 9-ounce package thin rice noodles
2 15-ounce cans Progresso® cannellini beans
4-ounce jar red curry paste
1-ounce package fresh basil

Staples

egg
cooking oil

Chicken Breasts with Cauliflower and Citrus

Citrus carries so much weight as a flavoring. A squeeze of lemon is often all you need for a piece of grilled fish or chicken. This recipe has a complex layering of citrus flavor that's easy to create because it uses shortcut foods like marmalade and grapefruit juice. –R

Tools

large sauté pan

Grocery List

Fresh

1¼ pounds chicken cutlets
1 head cauliflower
1 bunch chives

Packaged

12-ounce jar orange marmalade
64-ounce carton ruby red grapefruit juice

Staples

butter/flour
eggs
red wine vinegar

1. Heat a large sauté pan over medium heat. Add half the butter to the pan and heat until it's foamy but not brown. Season the chicken breasts on both sides with salt and pepper. Put the flour in a shallow dish. Dredge the chicken breasts in the flour, then dip in the beaten eggs to coat. Add the chicken to the pan and cook on both sides until golden brown and just cooked through, about 2 minutes.

2. Remove the chicken from the pan and keep it near the stove top so it stays warm. Add the cauliflower to the pan and cook until translucent, about 2 minutes. Add the marmalade, grapefruit juice, and vinegar, and stir until the marmalade dissolves. When mixture comes to a boil, swirl in the remaining butter and stir to make a smooth, silky sauce. Add the chicken back to the pan and spoon the sauce over it. Season to taste with salt and pepper, if necessary. Sprinkle the chives over the top and serve.

✱ If you can't buy chicken cutlets, you can make your own. See page 11 for directions.

Serves 4

1½	cups butter (3 sticks)
1¼	pounds chicken cutlets*
	Salt and freshly ground pepper
1	cup all-purpose flour
2	eggs, beaten well
2	cups very small cauliflower florets
½	cup orange marmalade
3	tablespoons ruby red grapefruit juice
2	tablespoons red wine vinegar
3	tablespoons chopped fresh chives

See photo, page 67.

Chicken with Lemon Butter, Thyme, & Pimientos

less than 15 minutes

Pimientos and peppers come in so many ready-to-eat, precooked, shortcut forms, it surprises me that anyone ever roasts and peels peppers from scratch. There are hundreds of pickled, roasted, and fried peppers out there—even pepper relishes—that rock. —R

Serves 4

12 tablespoons butter
   (1½ sticks), at room
   temperature
1 cup all-purpose flour
   Salt and freshly ground
   pepper
2 eggs, beaten well
4 thin chicken cutlets,
   about 5 ounces each*
½ cup fresh lemon juice
4 sprigs thyme
2 cups Mancini® sliced
   pimientos, drained

1. Heat 6 tablespoons of the butter in a large sauté pan over medium heat until it's foamy but not brown.

2. Meanwhile, in a shallow dish, season flour generously with salt and pepper. Have eggs in another shallow dish. Toss chicken in flour and then dip in the eggs. Add the chicken to the pan and sauté until light golden brown and cooked through, about 2 minutes per side.

3. Remove chicken from the pan and season with salt and pepper. Keep it on a platter near the stovetop so it stays warm.

4. Add the lemon juice to the pan and allow it to boil. Add the remaining butter, thyme, and pimientos. Cook, stirring occasionally, until sauce reduces slightly, 1 to 2 minutes. Season the sauce with salt and pepper.

5. Pour sauce liberally over the chicken and serve.

✱ If you can't buy chicken cutlets, you can make your own. See page 11 for directions.

Tools

large sauté pan

Grocery List

Fresh

4 5-ounce chicken cutlets

Packaged

1-ounce package fresh thyme
2 12-ounce jars Mancini®
sliced pimientos

Staples

butter
flour/eggs
lemons

Chicken with Turmeric & Onions

I call any sweet paste or puree a marmalade if it does what a marmalade does—add sweetness and texture to a dish. Turmeric might sound like a weird spice to put in marmalade, but it's great in sweet dishes or in savory dishes with sweet garnishes, like this. —R

Tools

large skillet

large sauté pan

Grocery List

Fresh

4 chicken breasts with skin

Packaged

Staples

extra-virgin olive oil
ground turmeric/honey
sweet onions

1. Heat a large skillet over high heat. Pour 2 tablespoons of the olive oil in the pan and let it get very hot. Season the skin side of the breasts generously with salt and pepper. Place chicken breasts in the hot pan skin side down. If the skin browns immediately, turn the pan down to medium-high heat. Let the breasts cook skin side down for about 8 minutes.

2. While the chicken is cooking, heat a large sauté pan over medium heat. Add the remaining 2 tablespoons olive oil and turmeric, and cook 1 minute. Add onions, stir to coat, and cook for 10 minutes, stirring frequently, until onions are light brown. Pour in the ¼ cup water, cover, reduce heat to low, and cook another 10 minutes until onions are very soft, stirring occasionally and adding a few spoons of additional water if the onions start to stick to the pan. Remove from heat and stir in honey. Season with salt and pepper to taste. Keep the onion marmalade warm until ready to serve.

3. When the chicken breasts are browned, season the side that's facing up with salt and pepper, and turn them over and cook them until they're done, about another 5 minutes. Serve chicken with the onion marmalade.

Serves 4

- 4 tablespoons Bertolli® extra-virgin olive oil
- 4 chicken breasts, skin on Salt and freshly ground pepper
- 1 tablespoon ground turmeric
- 2 large or 3 medium sweet onions, such as Vidalia, sliced thin
- ¼ cup water, plus more as needed
- 2 tablespoons honey

See photo, page 72.

Buttermilk-Battered **Fried Chicken**
with Mashed Potatoes and Cabbage

Why buttermilk-fried chicken? Buttermilk contains lactic acid, which tenderizes the chicken, gives it a great tangy taste, and reacts with the flour to form a crunchy crust. Soaking the chicken in it for a half hour will do the trick, but overnight is even better. —R

Serves 4

- 8 3-ounce chicken cutlets
- 1 quart buttermilk
- 1 quart canola oil
- 2 cups all-purpose flour
- 1 tablespoon cayenne pepper
  Salt and cracked black pepper
- 2 packages Diner's Choice® garlic mashed potatoes
- 1 cup drained sweet and sour cabbage, drained
- ½ cup fresh flat-leaf parsley, chopped
- 2 lemons, cut into wedges

1. In a shallow dish, submerge chicken completely in buttermilk. If you can, marinate for a half hour in the refrigerator.

2. In a large Dutch oven heat the canola oil to 400°F.

3. In another shallow dish, combine flour, cayenne pepper, and plenty of cracked pepper. Remove the chicken from the buttermilk and toss in the flour, coating it on all sides.

4. With a pair of tongs, gently lay the battered chicken in the oil. Move the cutlets around in the pot to make sure they are separated. The oil temperature will drop—maintain it at about 350°F. Fry for about 2 minutes or until chicken is golden brown, crispy, and just cooked through.

5. Pull the chicken out of oil and drain on a plate lined with paper towels; season well with salt.

6. Meanwhile, combine the mashed potatoes and the drained cabbage in a medium saucepan over medium-high heat. Stir often until hot, about 4 minutes. Sprinkle mashed potatoes and cabbage with parsley. Serve chicken with the mashed potatoes and cabbage and the lemon wedges on the side.

Tools

Dutch oven

medium saucepan

Grocery List

Fresh

8 3-ounce chicken cutlets
1 bunch flat-leaf parsley

Packaged

1 quart buttermilk
2 packages Diner's Choice®
garlic mashed potatoes
16-ounce container sweet and
sour cabbage

Staples

canola oil/flour
cayenne pepper
lemons

Quick **Chicken Stew** with Tomatoes and Mustard

Paprika is one of those spices that sits in the cupboard for three generations before someone moves and throws it out. Don't let that happen. If you like peppers, you'll like paprika. Expand your horizons and try this Spanish smoked paprika. —R

Tools

Dutch oven

Grocery List

Fresh

2 pounds boneless chicken (breasts and thighs)
1 bunch flat-leaf parsley

Packaged

3.15-ounce tube Amore® garlic paste
15-ounce can plum tomatoes in tomato puree
2 15-ounce cans Progresso® cannellini beans
2.10-ounce bottle Spanish smoked paprika

Staples

extra-virgin olive oil
chicken broth
Dijon mustard

1. In a Dutch oven or heavy-bottomed pot, heat olive oil over high heat.

2. Season chicken generously with salt and pepper. Brown the chicken in the oil. (You may need to do this in batches.) Return all of the chicken to the pot and add the garlic to the oil; cook until fragrant, about 1 minute. Pour in the broth and bring to a simmer. Whisk in the mustard.

3. Pour tomatoes and puree into a bowl. Gently crush them with your hands.

4. Add tomatoes, beans, and paprika to the chicken. Cover with a lid and simmer for about 10 minutes.

5. Sprinkle with parsley and serve.

Serves 4

- 3 tablespoons Bertolli® extra-virgin olive oil
- 2 pounds boneless chicken (combination of thighs and breasts), cut into small chunks
  Salt and freshly ground pepper
- 3 tablespoons Amore® garlic paste or 9 garlic cloves, chopped
- 1 cup chicken broth
- ½ cup Dijon mustard
- 1 15-ounce can plum tomatoes in tomato puree
- 2 15-ounce cans Progresso® cannellini beans, rinsed and drained
- 1 tablespoon Spanish smoked paprika (also called pimenton)
- ½ cup fresh flat-leaf parsley, chopped

Warm **Chicken & Bacon** Salad

less than 15
minutes

Great, fresh-tasting rotisserie chicken is available just about
everywhere. I think it's one of the most underutilized foods out
there. A perfectly roasted chicken can be turned into many, many
dishes. –R

Serves 4

1   fully cooked rotisserie
    chicken, about 3 pounds
    (if that's unavailable, use
    2 10-ounce packages
    Perdue® ready-to-eat
    roasted chicken)
1   pound thick-cut bacon,
    cut into small pieces
6   tablespoons B&G® hot dog
    relish
⅔   cup Hellman's®
    Dijonnaise™
1   10-ounce package Dole®
    chopped romaine
    Salt and freshly black
    ground pepper

1. Keep the rotisserie chicken warm in a 200°F
oven, if necessary. When ready to make the
salad, tear the chicken into large bite-size pieces,
removing all the bones. Place in a large bowl.

2. Heat a large sauté pan over medium heat. Add
the bacon and cook until soft and light brown.
Drain on a paper towel-lined plate.

3. Add the bacon, hot dog relish, and Dijonnaise
to the chicken. Mix well. Add the lettuce and
season to taste with salt and pepper. Divide salad
among four plates and serve.

Tools

large sauté pan

Grocery List

Fresh

1 pound thick-cut bacon

Packaged

3-pound rostisserie chicken
10-ounce jar B&G® hot dog
relish
2 8-ounce jars Hellman's®
Dijonnaise™
10-ounce package Dole®
chopped romaine

Staples

Red Ginger **Chicken Satay**

I call this "red ginger" because I had a cousin named "Red," and he was called that because his hair was the color of "ginger." I am almost certain that Red never ate anything like this dish—but I know he'd like people to think he did. –R

Tools

grill pan

1. In a large bowl mix together garlic, pineapple juice, sugar, ginger, peanut butter, and vinegar. Marinate chicken in ¾ of the mixture for about 30 minutes. Thread cubed chicken onto skewers.

2. Preheat a grill/grill pan/broiler on high. Cook chicken skewers for about 8 minutes or until cooked through, turning occasionally.

3. In a medium bowl toss the sliced cucumbers with the remaining marinade. Serve chicken on a bed of the dressed cucumber slices. Garnish with sliced tomatoes, lime wedges, cilantro, and crushed red pepper, if desired.

Serves 4

- 2 teaspoons Amore® garlic paste or 2 garlic cloves, chopped
- 1 cup pineapple juice
- 1 tablespoon sugar
- 2 teaspoons finely chopped ginger
- 6 tablespoons creamy peanut butter
- 2 teaspoons red wine vinegar
- 2 pounds boneless, skinless chicken breast, cut into cubes
- 16 bamboo skewers, soaked in water for 30 minutes
- 2 seedless cucumbers, peeled and sliced
  Sliced tomatoes, lime wedges, cilantro, and crushed red pepper, for garnish (optional)

See photo, page 177.

Grocery List

Fresh

3-inch piece ginger
2 pounds boneless, skinless chicken breasts
2 seedless cucumbers

Packaged

3.15-ounce tube Amore® garlic paste
2 6-ounce cans pineapple juice
1 package bamboo skewers

Staples

sugar/garlic
peanut butter
red wine vinegar

Chicken with Garlic & Spaghetti

less than 30 minutes

Italians don't typically put chunks of chicken in a pasta dish. If meat is part of the dish, it's usually a tough cut that's been simmered into submission for hours until it's a rich, deeply flavorful, and tender ragu—but who has time for that six nights a week? —R

Serves 4

1 tablespoon salt
1 pound dried spaghetti
2 cups frozen green peas
1½ pounds chicken tender
3 ounces garlic-infused olive oil (I like Consorzio)
A handful of whole flat-leaf parsley leaves
A handful of freshly grated Parmigiano-Reggiano cheese

1. In a stockpot or Dutch oven, boil 5 quarts of water. When it boils, add the salt. Add the spaghetti to the water and stir it continuously for 2 minutes. Cook it another 4 minutes, or until when you bite a piece you see a thin ring of white uncooked pasta in the center of the spaghetti strand. Add the chicken and peas to the pasta water and bring water back to a simmer. Simmer for 2 minutes. Drain the pasta, peas, and chicken.

2. Heat a large sauté pan over medium heat. Add the garlic oil and let it get hot. Add the parsley leaves and let them sizzle for a second or two, then add the drained pasta, peas, and chicken.

3. Toss the pasta in the pan for about 2 minutes. Season to taste with salt, pepper, and Parmigiano.

Tools

stockpot

large sauté pan

Grocery List

Fresh

1½ pounds chicken tenders
1 bunch flat-leaf parsley

Packaged

1 pound spaghetti
8.1-ounce garlic-infused olive oil
10-ounce package frozen peas

Staples

Parmigiano-Reggiano cheese

Creamy **Parmesan Risotto**
with Chicken & Mushrooms

There are very few things I love to cook more than risotto. I love it for the same reason most people hate cooking it: It's a long process—but it's so delicious, we keep trying. I have made it a very simple process here without sacrificing flavor in any way. —R

Tools

large sauté pan

1. Heat a large sauté pan over high heat. When it's hot, pour the oil into the pan and let it get really hot. Season the chicken with salt and pepper. Add the chicken to the pan and sauté for 2 minutes, or until chicken browns a little.

2. Add the onion and mushrooms to the pan and sauté for another 3 minutes. Add the wine and cook until it has reduced by half, about 2 minutes. Add the rice and cook and stir until everything is mixed. Add the chicken broth and bring to a boil. Cover and let it sit for 5 minutes.

3. Stir in the cheese until rice is creamy. Season with salt and pepper to taste. Stir in the parsley and serve.

Serves 4

½ cup Bertolli® extra-virgin olive oil

1½ pounds chicken breasts, cut into chunks

Salt and freshly ground pepper

1 medium red onion, chopped

1 16-ounce package of portobello mushrooms, cleaned and roughly chopped

½ cup dry white wine

3 cups Minute® rice

2½ cups chicken broth

½ cup freshly grated Parmigiano-Reggiano cheese

¼ cup roughly chopped fresh flat-leaf parsley

Grocery List

Fresh

1½ pounds chicken breasts
1 bunch flat-leaf parsley

Packaged

16-ounce package portobello mushrooms
14-ounce box Minute® rice

Staples

red onion
extra-virgin olive oil
dry white wine/chicken broth
Parmigiano-Reggiano cheese

Chicken Braised with Paprika & Dijon

On a trip to Spain in 1997, I fell in love with paprika, both the smoked and regular varieties. It's often thought of as exotic, but it's just dried and ground peppers. In this easy braise, mustard, tomato, and paprika create an ethereal flavor combination. —R

Serves 4

- 3 tablespoons Bertolli® extra-virgin olive oil
- 4 large boneless chicken breasts, with skin, each cut in half
  Salt and freshly ground pepper
- 1 tablespoon Amore® garlic paste or 3 garlic cloves, chopped
- 1 tablespoon paprika
- ½ cup sweet red or white wine
- 1 cup chicken broth
- 1 8-ounce can tomato sauce
- ¾ cup Dijon mustard
- ½ cup chopped fresh flat-leaf parsley

1. Heat a Dutch oven over high heat. Add the oil to the pan and let it get hot. Season the chicken generously with salt and pepper and add half of it to the pan. Allow it to brown, about 4 to 5 minutes, turning once. Remove chicken from the pan and repeat with remaining chicken. Return all of the chicken to the pot and add the garlic; cook and stir until it's fragrant, about 1 minute.

2. Add the paprika to the chicken and cook for 30 seconds or until paprika becomes fragrant. Add the wine to the pan and stir, scraping up any flavorful brown bits from the bottom of the pan. Cook, stirring occasionally, until the pan is nearly dry. Add the chicken broth and tomato sauce. Cover the pot and bring mixture to a boil. Lower the heat to a low simmer and braise the chicken for about 10 minutes or until it's cooked through.

3. Remove the chicken from the pan. Whisk in the mustard and bring the sauce to a simmer. Place 2 pieces of chicken on each plate and ladle plenty of sauce over them. Sprinkle with parsley and serve.

Tools

Dutch oven

Grocery List

Fresh

4 large boneless chicken breasts with skin
1 bunch flat-laf parsley

Packaged

3.15-ounce tube Amore® garlic paste
750 ml bottle sweet red or white wine

Staples

extra-virgin olive oil
paprika/tomato sauce
chicken broth/Dijon mustard

less than 30 minutes

Chicken-Fried **Turkey Steak**
with Walnut & Ricotta Gravy

As you might know, chicken–fried steak isn't made with chicken and most of the time the steak it *is* made with is barely recognizable. I'm thinking we should dress up some turkey and reinterpret gravy in a way that would make my mama proud. —R

Tools

food processor

large sauté pan

Grocery List

Fresh

1½ pounds thin turkey cutlets

Packaged

8-ounce bag walnuts
3.15-ounce tube Amore® garlic paste
15-ounce container ricotta

Staples

white bread/flour
extra-virgin olive oil
cooking oil

1. Soak the bread in cold water for 2 minutes.

2. Squeeze out the bread and put it in a food processor. Add the walnuts and garlic. Chop until a smooth paste is formed (some walnut chunks are all right). Transfer to a bowl and add the ricotta and olive oil. Mix well and season with salt and pepper.

3. Put the flour in a shallow dish and season it with salt and pepper. Dredge the cutlets in the seasoned flour, shaking off any excess.

4. Heat a large sauté pan or cast-iron skillet over medium-high heat. When the pan is hot, add the cooking oil and allow it to get very hot. Carefully place half of the cutlets in the oil and fry until cooked through—it should take about 2 minutes per side. Remove the cooked cutlets from the pan and keep them on a platter next to the stovetop so they stay warm. Repeat with the other half of the cutlets.

5. Place 2 steaks on each of four plates and top with the walnut and ricotta gravy.

Serves 4

2 slices white bread
1 cup walnuts, toasted
1 tablespoon Amore® garlic paste or 3 garlic cloves, peeled
1 cup ricotta
2 tablespoons Bertolli® extra-virgin olive oil
Salt and freshly ground pepper
2 cups all-purpose flour
1½ pounds thin turkey cutlets, about 8 4-ounce pieces
¼ cup cooking oil

Chopped **Turkey Steaks**, Italian Style

When I worked as a pantry cook at the New Hyde Park Inn, I nearly always picked "chopped steak" to eat on my dinner break. I liked the idea of eating "steak." At 14, ground meat formed into steaks and broiled was good enough for me—and it still is. —R

Serves 4

1 pound ground turkey
½ cup Progresso® Italian-style breadcrumbs
2 eggs, lightly beaten
3 tablespoons water
¼ cup finely grated Parmesan cheese
¼ teaspoon crushed red pepper
2 tablespoons chopped fresh flat-leaf parsley
Salt and freshly ground pepper
Nonstick vegetable spray
2 large ripe beefsteak tomatoes, cut into 4 thick slices each

1. Preheat oven to 450°F.

2. In a large bowl, combine turkey, breadcrumbs, eggs, water, cheese, red pepper, and parsley. Season with salt and pepper. Mix with a wooden spoon until all the ingredients are well incorporated. Form into four flat ovals and place on a rimmed baking sheet coated with nonstick vegetable spray.

3. Place two tomato slices on the top of each chopped steak and season with salt and pepper.

4. Put in the oven and cook for 10 minutes, or until the internal temperature is 155°F. Remove the steaks from the oven and turn the oven to broil. Place the steaks under the broiler for 3 to 5 minutes, or until the tomatoes begin to sizzle. Serve with tomato juices drizzled on top.

Tools

rimmed baking sheet

Grocery List

Fresh

1 pound ground turkey
1 bunch flat-leaf parsley
2 large beefsteak tomatoes

Packaged

Staples

breadcrumbs
eggs/Parmesan cheese
crushed red pepper
nonstick vegetable spray

less than 30
minutes

Curried Turkey Fricassee

Fricassee is just a fancy French word for stew. But unlike a real stew, a fricassee doesn't require cooking tough cuts of meat for a long time. A fricassee is usually cooked quickly with tender cuts of meat. The word fricassee just has a nice ring to it, doesn't it? —R

Tools

medium saucepan

very large sauté pan

Grocery List

Fresh

1½ pounds turkey breast
1 bunch cilantro

Packaged

14-ounce box Minute® rice
1 16-ounce package frozen cauliflower
16-ounce jar Aunt Nellie's® pickled beets
6-ounce carton whole-milk plain yogurt

Staples

butter
curry powder

1. In a medium saucepan bring water (lightly salted) to a boil. Stir in rice, turn off heat, and allow rice to absorb the liquid for 5 minutes.

2. Heat the butter in a very large sauté pan over medium-low heat. Add the curry powder and stir until the powder is completely blended with the butter. Add the cauliflower and beets and bring to a simmer. Stir and cook until the liquid thickens to a soup consistency. Add the turkey chunks to the pan and simmer just until cooked, about 5 minutes. Season with salt and pepper to taste. Turn off the heat and stir in the yogurt and cilantro.

3. Fluff the rice and divide it among four plates. Spoon an equal amount of curry mixture over each bed of rice and serve.

Serves 4

1½ cups water
2   cups Minute® rice
4   tablespoons butter
1   tablespoon curry powder
2   cups frozen, cooked cauliflower florets
2   cups sliced Aunt Nellie's® pickled beets, drained
1¼ pounds turkey breast, cut into medium-sized chunks
Salt and freshly black ground pepper
¼   cup whole-milk plain yogurt
½   cup fresh cilantro, chopped

Turkey & Prosciutto Rolls with Escarole

Delicate herbs like basil, cilantro, and parsley are best used fresh. Hardy herbs like thyme, rosemary, and oregano dry with their flavor mostly intact. I call for fresh oregano because it is usually better, but dry works fine—use one-fourth of the fresh quantity. –R

Serves 4

8   2-ounce thin turkey cutlets
    Salt and freshly ground pepper
4   teaspoons Amore® garlic paste or 4 garlic cloves, chopped
4   sprigs fresh oregano
8   thin slices prosciutto (about 2 ounces)
4   ounces provolone, sliced into 8 thin pieces
1   cup Bertolli® extra-virgin olive oil
¼   cup red wine vinegar
4   cups washed and roughly chopped escarole

1. Preheat a grill/grill pan/broiler on high.

2. Lay pieces of turkey on a flat work surface. Season with salt and pepper.

3. On half of each piece of turkey, place 1 teaspoon of the chopped garlic and 1 sprig of the oregano leaves. (The turkey will be folded in half to create a 3x3-inch square, so the filling must be layered on half of each piece only. Do not over-stuff the turkey because the filling will come out the sides when grilling.) Place a slice of prosciutto and a slice of provolone over the garlic and oregano.

4. Fold the empty half over the stuffing. Stick a toothpick all the way through the center. Repeat with remaining turkey cutlets. Brush each roll with a few drops of olive oil and sprinkle with salt and pepper. Grill rolls until golden brown and cooked through, about 3 minutes per side.

5. Meanwhile, in a large mixing bowl combine the olive oil and red wine vinegar and toss in the escarole leaves. Season to taste. Serve turkey rolls with escarole salad. (Remember to take out the toothpicks.)

Tools

grill pan

Grocery List

Fresh

8 2-ounce thin turkey cutlets
1 head escarole

Packaged

3.15-ounce tube Amore® garlic paste
1-ounce package fresh oregano
2-ounce package prosciutto
8-ounce package provolone cheese

Staples

extra-virgin olive oil
red wine vinegar

Turkey Breasts with Apricot & Grapefruit Glaze

Citrus fruits have different levels of acidity, so I like to blend them and adjust their flavors with vinegar and something sweet. Experiment and create your own mix for this recipe. Orange or lemon juice would be equally good. –R

Tools

very large sauté pan

Grocery List

Fresh

1¼ pounds thin turkey cutlets
1 bunch chives

Packaged

12-ounce jar apricot marmalade
64-ounce carton ruby red grapefruit juice

Staples

butter
eggs/flour
red wine vinegar

1. Heat 1 tablespoon of the butter in a very large sauté pan over medium-low heat. Place flour in a shallow dish. Dredge turkey breasts in the flour and then dip in the beaten eggs, turning to coat. Add half of the turkey cutlets to the pan and cook on both sides until golden brown and cooked through, about 2 minutes per side. Remove from the pan and season with salt and pepper. Keep on a platter near the stove top so they stay warm. Add another tablespoon of butter to the pan and repeat with the remaining cutlets.

2. Drain all but 1 tablespoon of butter and drippings from the pan. Add the marmalade and allow it to dissolve over medium-low heat. Stir in grapefruit juice and vinegar and bring to a boil. When mixture comes to a boil, turn off the heat and swirl in the remaining 2 tablespoons butter. Add all of the turkey back to the pan and baste with the sauce. Season to taste with salt and pepper, if necessary. Sprinkle chives on top and serve.

✱ If you can't buy turkey cutlets, you can make your own. See page 11 for directions.

Serves 4

4   tablespoons butter
3   cups all-purpose flour
1¼ pounds thin turkey cutlets*
2   eggs, well beaten
    Salt and freshly ground pepper
½   cup apricot marmalade
3   tablespoons ruby red grapefruit juice
1   tablespoon red wine vinegar
3   tablespoons chopped fresh chives

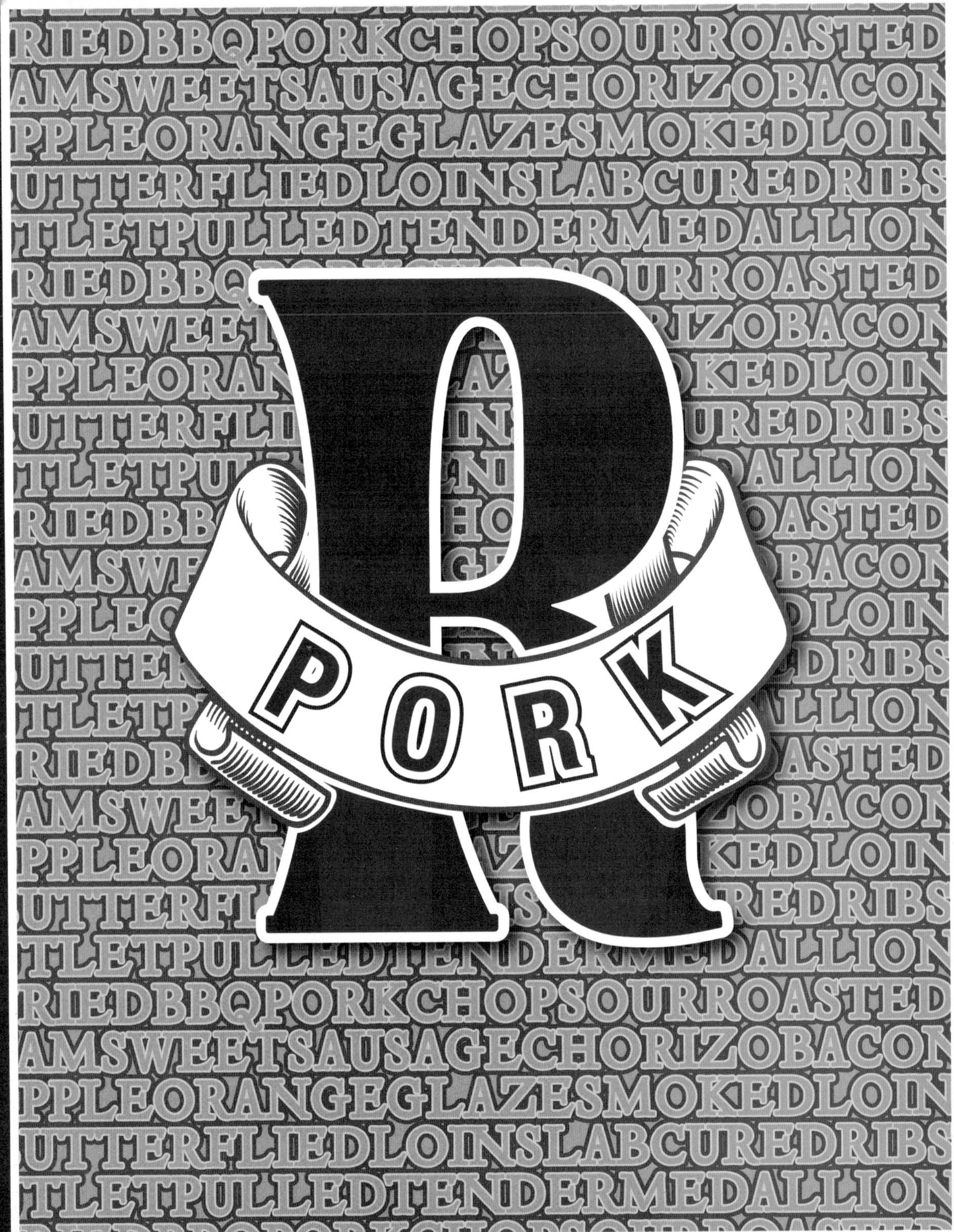
PORK

"The most important cooking tool is your palate. The only difference between a good cook and a great cook is how much they taste their food before serving it."

Orange and Cinnamon-Glazed
Pork Tenderloin

Salad greens such as radicchio, endive, escarole, chicory, and friseé are also good cooked and served warm as a vegetable—with the exception of iceberg lettuce (although I am sure that someone out there could make a compelling case for cooked iceberg). —R

Tools

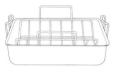

roasting pan and rack

Grocery List

Fresh

1½-pound pork tenderloin
4 heads radicchio

Packaged

16-ounce can frozen orange juice concentrate

Staples

ground cinnamon

1. Preheat the oven to 450°F.

2. To make the glaze, combine the orange juice concentrate, cinnamon, and salt and pepper to taste in a large bowl. Reserve ½ cup of the glaze. Submerge the tenderloin in the remaining glaze and let it sit at room temperature for 10 minutes.

3. Put the tenderloin on a roasting rack in a roasting pan and pour the glaze over it, allowing it to fall through the roasting rack to the bottom of the roasting pan. Season tenderloin with salt and pepper. Roast for 15 minutes (the glaze should begin to bubble and brown at this point). Add the radicchio to the pan and roast for another 5 minutes.

4. Remove from the oven and allow to rest 5 minutes. Drizzle 2 tablespoons per serving of the reserved glaze over the radicchio. Slice the tenderloin and serve with the radicchio wedges.

Serves 4

- 2 cups frozen orange juice concentrate, thawed
- 1 tablespoon ground cinnamon
  Salt and freshly ground pepper
- 1 whole pork tenderloin, about 1½ pounds
- 4 heads radicchio, quartered

Fried **Pork Cutlets** with Chopped Salad

less than 15 minutes

Veal Milanese is a breaded, pan-fried veal chop served with some kind of salad on top. Pork makes a great substitute for the veal in this Milanese-style dish. And call me unsophisticated, but I think nothing will do in a "chopped salad" like crunchy iceberg. —R

Serves 4

1	cup cooking oil
1	cup all-purpose flour
2	eggs, beaten
1	cup plain breadcrumbs
	Salt and freshly ground pepper
4	8-ounce boneless pork loin chops, pounded thin
½	cup of your favorite garlic and herb vinaigrette
1	head radicchio, cored and chopped
1	head iceberg lettuce, cored and chopped
¼	pound provolone, diced

See photo, page 72.

1. Heat ½ cup oil in each of 2 large sauté pans over high heat.

2. Place the flour, beaten eggs, and breadcrumbs in three separate shallow dishes. Season the flour with salt and pepper.

3. Season each chop with salt and pepper. With your left hand, dredge each chop in the flour, shaking off excess. With your right hand, dip each chop into the beaten eggs. Finally, with your left hand, dredge the chops in the breadcrumbs. Use your dry (left) hand to press the crumbs into the chops. Gently shake off any excess crumbs.

4. Carefully lay 2 chops in each pan with the hot oil. The chops should sizzle immediately and begin to brown.

5. Meanwhile, in a large mixing bowl, drizzle the vinaigrette over the radicchio, lettuce, and provolone. Toss the salad and season with salt and pepper.

6. Turn the chops over when brown on one side, about 2 to 3 minutes. When golden brown and fully cooked (it's OK to look), remove chops from pans and drain on a paper towel-lined plate.

7. Place chops on four plates and top each with some of the chopped salad.

Tools

2 large sauté pans

Grocery List

Fresh

4 8-ounce boneless pork loin chops
1 head radicchio
1 head iceberg lettuce

Packaged

8-ounce container Progresso® breadcrumbs
16-ounce bottle garlic and herb vinaigrette
8-ounce package provolone

Staples

cooking oil
all-purpose flour
eggs

Mexican Pork with Okra

Okra inspires delight in some—and in others, not so much. I understand both reactions. It's one of those foods that—if not prepared properly—can make even the adventuresome flee the pot. For everyday use, I recommend buying canned okra. —R

Tools

large sauté pan

Grocery List

Fresh

1½ pounds boneless pork stew meat

Packaged

1.25-ounce package taco seasoning mix
8.25-ounce can Doña Maria® mole adobo sauce
14-ounce can Allen's® cut okra

Staples

cooking oil
honey
onion

1. Heat a large sauté pan over high heat. When it's hot, add the oil and allow it to get very hot.

2. Season the pork with salt and pepper and add it to the pan. Cook, stirring occasionally, until the pork begins to brown, about 3 to 4 minutes. Add the onion and sauté until it begins to soften. Add taco seasoning, adobo sauce, honey, and okra. Stir the mixture and bring it to a simmer. Simmer for about 5 minutes, until sauce begins to thicken, and serve.

Serves 4

2   tablespoons cooking oil
1½ pounds boneless pork stew meat, cut into 1-inch cubes
    Salt and freshly ground pepper
1   large onion, diced
1½ teaspoons taco seasoning mix
2   tablespoons Doña Maria® mole adobo sauce
2   tablespoons honey
1   14-ounce can Allen's® cut okra

103

Grilled **Pork Chops** and Peppers alla Brace

less than 15 minutes

The phrase *alla brace* is Italian and refers to those bright red embers that bring so much flavor to the table when you cook over coals. I know you can't always cook over a charcoal grill, but do it with this dish if you can. —R

Serves 4

6 tablespoons Bertolli® extra-virgin olive oil

3 tablespoons chopped fresh flat-leaf parsley

2 teaspoons chopped fresh rosemary

1 teaspoon crushed red pepper

3 tablespoons red wine vinegar

Salt and freshly ground pepper

8 boneless thin-cut pork loin chops

4 Cubanelle peppers, quartered

See photo, page 68.

1. Preheat a grill over high heat. Use wood or charcoal, if available.

2. Meanwhile, in a large bowl combine olive oil, parsley, rosemary, red pepper, and vinegar. Season with salt and pepper.

3. Add the pork and peppers to the bowl, turning to coat everything well, and and allow to marinate at room temperature for 10 minutes.

4. Put the pork chops and peppers in a grill basket. Grill until the pork reaches an internal temperature of 155°F and the peppers are charred and soft, about 3 to 4 minutes per side.

Tools

grill basket

Grocery List

Fresh

1 bunch flat-leaf parsley
8 boneless thin-cut pork loin chops
4 Cubanelle peppers

Packaged

1-ounce pckage fresh rosemary

Staples

extra-virgin olive oil
red wine vinegar
crushed red pepper

Grilled **Pork Chops** with Miso & Apple Dressing

Crisp, light, fresh salads are wonderful with grilled or broiled meats. Dinner for me is often a big green salad with an interesting dressing and a few broiled pork chops, steak, or boneless salmon steaks. Create variety by using different types of greens. –R

1. In a large bowl, combine vinegar, miso, applesauce, vermouth, and olive oil. Set aside.

2. Meanwhile heat a grill/grill pan/broiler on high until very hot. Season the pork chops with salt and pepper and brush a tiny bit of the dressing on both sides of each chop. Grill until fully cooked, about 3 minutes per side. (Allow the dressing to char slightly.)

3. Add salad greens to remaining dressing in bowl and toss to combine. Serve pork chops with salad.

Serves 4

3	tablespoon rice wine vinegar
1	teaspoon miso paste (light is best, but any kind will do)
1	teaspoon smooth applesauce
2	tablespoons Martini & Rossi® rosso vermouth
1	tablespoon Bertolli® extra-virgin olive oil
2	pounds boneless thin-cut pork loin chops (about 8 pieces)
	Salt and freshly ground pepper
1	10-ounce bag Dole® Italian Salad blend

Tools

grill pan

Grocery List

Fresh

2 pounds boneless thin-cut pork loin chops

Packaged

6-ounce container miso paste
4-ounce container applesauce
750 ml bottle Martini & Rossi® rosso vermouth
10-ounce bag Dole® Italian salad blend

Staples

rice wine vinegar
extra-virgin olive oil

Pork Chops Puttanesca

The genesis of "puttanesca" varies depending on who tells it to you but it's always a colorful story. Most versions affiliate it with Italian "ladies of the night" (singular: "puttana"), who made a spicy sauce with hot peppers, capers, and olives to tempt their customers. –R

Serves 4

1   14-ounce jar Victoria®
    puttanesca sauce
1   teaspoon crushed red
    pepper flakes
2   teaspoons capers, drained
1   2-ounce can sliced black
    olives
8   boneless thin-cut pork
    loin chops
1   tube refrigerated polenta,
    cut into 8 1-inch rounds
2   tablespoons Bertolli®
    extra-virgin olive oil
    Salt and freshly ground
    pepper
3   tablespoons chopped
    flat-leaf parsley

    See photo, page 77.

1. Preheat a grill/grill pan/broiler on high.

2. Meanwhile, heat a large saucepan over high heat. Add the puttanesca sauce, red pepper flakes, capers, and olives, and bring to a boil. Reduce heat to medium-low and bring sauce to a simmer; cover.

3. While the sauce is simmering, brush pork chops and polenta rounds with the olive oil and season both with salt and pepper on both sides. Grill pork and polenta 3 to 4 minutes on each side. The polenta should be browned on the outside and the pork should have an internal temperature of 155°F.

4. Top polenta and pork chops with lots of sauce. Sprinkle with parsley and serve.

Tools

grill pan

large saucepan

Grocery List

Fresh

8 boneless thin-cut pork loin
chops
1 bunch flat-leaf parsley

Packaged

14-ounce jar Victoria®
puttanesca sauce
2-ounce can sliced black olives
16-ounce tube refrigerated
polenta

Staples

crushed red pepper flakes
capers
extra-virgin olive oil

Pork Pot Roast with Artichoke & Peppers

Why put bacon and other cuts of pork together in a dish? I love the smoky/salty flavor and rich texture of the bacon. It helps reinforce the flavor of the uncured pork and adds new flavors to the dish without overwhelming it. —R

Tools

very large sauté pan

Grocery List

Fresh

¼ pound bacon
2 pounds pork stew meat

Packaged

3.15-ounce tube Amore® garlic paste
12-ounce jar quartered marinated artichoke hearts
14-ounce jar Mancini® roasted red peppers
18-ounce jar Victoria® Fra Diavolo sauce

Staples

1. Heat a very large sauté pan over high heat. Add the bacon to the pan and quickly stir it. When the bacon starts to soften and become translucent, remove it from the pan.

2. Season the pork with salt and pepper and brown, stirring occasionally, in the rendered bacon fat, about 4 minutes. Add the garlic and sauté, stirring, for 1 minute. Add the artichokes, peppers, and Fra Diavolo sauce. Add the bacon back to the pan and stir to combine. Bring to a boil, lower the heat, and simmer, covered, for 15 minutes.

3. Serve pork with plenty of sauce.

Serves 4

¼ pound bacon, cut into small strips

2 pounds pork stew meat (already cut into large chunks)

Salt and freshly ground pepper

3 tablespoons Amore® garlic paste or 9 cloves garlic, chopped

1 12-ounce jar quartered marinated artichoke hearts

1 14-ounce jar Mancini® roasted red peppers

1 18-ounce jar Victoria® Fra Diavolo sauce

Grilled **Pork Chops** & Beans

I am always looking for great short cut foods. I love the garlic paste from Amore®. It's really convenient and tastes almost like fresh chopped garlic. It's also very easy to portion because it's squeezed out of a tube like toothpaste. Very cool. —R

Serves 4

¼ cup Amore® garlic paste or 12 cloves garlic, chopped

2 tablespoons chopped fresh rosemary

2 tablespoons Bertolli® extra-virgin olive oil

Salt and freshly ground pepper

8 thin-cut pork loin chops

¼ pound bacon, cut into medium-sized chunks (about ⅓ cup)

3 cups fresh white button mushrooms, stems removed, sliced

¼ cup ketchup

2 14-ounce cans Progresso® kidney beans, rinsed and drained

1. Preheat grill/grill pan/broiler on high.

2. In a small bowl combine half the garlic paste with half of the rosemary and 1 tablespoon of the olive oil. Season with salt and pepper. Rub the seasoned garlic paste onto both sides of the pork chops. Place chops on the grill and cook until the internal temperature is 155°F, about 3 to 4 minutes on each side.

3. Meanwhile, heat the remaining olive oil in a medium saucepan over high heat. Add the bacon and cook until it begins to soften. Add the mushrooms, season with salt and pepper, and cook for 2 minutes. Add the remaining garlic, rosemary, and ketchup, and stir until mixed well. Add the beans and bring to a simmer. Cook for about 5 minutes or until heated through.

4. Serve pork chops with seasoned beans.

Tools

grill pan

medium saucepan

Grocery List

Fresh

8 thin-cut pork chops
¼ pound bacon
3 cups white button mushrooms

Packaged

3.15-ounce tube Amore® garlic paste
1-ounce package fresh rosemary
2 14-ounce cans Progresso® kidney beans

Staples

extra-virgin olive oil
ketchup

less than 30
minutes

Grilled Pork with Cherry Tomatoes & Mustard

Balsamic vinegar is made from white grape juice that has been boiled down and reduced, fermented, and then aged in wooden casks. With all that goes into the making of it, you can see why it makes such a flavor impact in the sauce for these chops. –R

Tools

grill pan

large sauté pan

Grocery List

Fresh

8 thin-cut boneless pork loin chops
2 pints cherry or pear tomatoes

Packaged

10-ounce package Dole® classic romaine

Staples

extra-virgin olive oil
red onion/Dijon mustard
balsamic vinegar

1. Preheat a grill/grill pan/broiler on high. Season pork chops with salt and pepper. Grill chops for 3 to 4 minutes per side, or until done to your preference.

2. Heat a large sauté pan over medium heat. When warm, add the olive oil. Add onion and cook, stirring occasionally, until it begins to soften, about 3 to 4 minutes. Add the tomatoes and cook, stirring gently, until they're just warmed through, about 1 to 2 minutes. Remove the onion and tomatoes from the heat and stir in the mustard and vinegar.

3. In a large bowl, toss the tomato mixture with the salad greens. Season to taste with salt and pepper and serve alongside the grilled chops.

Serves 4

8   thin-cut boneless pork loin chops
    Salt and freshly ground pepper
2   tablespoons Bertolli® extra-virgin olive oil
1   large red onion, diced
2   pints very small cherry or pear tomatoes
3   tablespoons Dijon mustard
2   teaspoons balsamic vinegar
3   cups Dole® classic romaine

Pork Chops Stuffed with Portobello Mushrooms

Pigs have been bred to be very lean in the last 30 years. To compensate, I created this stuffing with juicy mushrooms and goat cheese. It makes a very lean pork chop seem very rich. It's a nice surprise to cut into something that has a yummy, cheesy center. –R

Serves 4

½ cup Bertolli® extra-virgin olive oil

4 large portobello mushrooms, stemmed and sliced thin (about 7 ounces)

8 ounces goat cheese, softened
 Salt and freshly ground pepper

4 pork loin chops, about 1½ inches thick

2 tablespoons butter

1 medium Vidalia onion

½ cup water

2 heads frisée lettuce, roughly torn

1. Heat a large sauté pan over high heat. When it's hot add 3 tablespoons of the olive oil to the pan. When the oil is hot, add the mushrooms and cook, stirring occasionally, until golden brown, about 2 to 3 minutes. Take the pan off the heat. Fold the goat cheese into the warm mushrooms and season to taste with salt and pepper.

2. Using the tip of a very sharp paring knife, make a slit halfway up the side of the chop to create a pocket. Divide the mushroom mixture among the four chops, stuffing evenly and neatly.

3. Wipe out the sauté pan with a clean paper towel. Heat ⅓ cup of the olive oil in the pan over medium heat. Add the chops and cook until golden brown on both sides and just cooked through, about 5 to 7 minutes per side.

4. While the pork is cooking, heat a second large sauté pan over very high heat. Add the butter and immediately add the onion. Allow onion to char and become mostly tender, about 5 minutes. Season with salt and pepper. Add a little water to the pan, stirring to loosen any onion that is sticking to the pan.

5. In a large bowl, toss torn frisée with remaining olive oil. Season to taste with salt and pepper.

6. Serve chops with onion sauce and frisée salad.

Tools

2 large sauté pans

Grocery List

Fresh

4 large portobello mushrooms
4 pork loin chops
2 heads frisée lettuce

Packaged

8-ounce log goat cheese

Staples

extra-virgin olive oil
butter
Vidalia onion

Grilled Pork Chops
with Cumin-Scented Fricassee of Tomatoes

The warm aroma and flavor of cumin gives it an appeal that isn't difficult to grasp. It's so intense and distinctive that it really needs no backup. It's traditionally paired with tomatoes in Moroccan food because the two are so good to each other. (You'll see.) –R

1. Preheat a grill/grill pan/broiler on high.

2. Mix 2 tablespoons of the olive oil with 2 cloves of the chopped garlic (or 1 tablespoon of the garlic paste). Rub this mixture onto the entire surface of both sides of the pork chops. Season the chops generously with salt and pepper. Place chops on the grill and cook for about 7 minutes per side. Remove from grill and allow to rest, lightly covered with foil, for about 4 to 5 minutes.

3. While the pork is cooking and resting, make the fricassee. Heat ¼ cup of the olive oil in a large sauté pan over medium heat. Add the onions and the remaining 2 cloves of chopped garlic (or 1 tablespoon of garlic paste). Season the onions and garlic with salt and pepper to taste and cook, stirring occasionally, for about 7 minutes. When the onions begin to soften, add the cumin, chopped tomatoes, and reserved tomato puree. Simmer this mixture for about 10 more minutes, or until onions are completely tender and much of the liquid has evaporated.

4. Divide the fricassee among four large bowls. Place pork chops atop the fricassee. Drizzle the chops with a little bit of olive oil, if desired. Sprinkle with cilantro and serve.

Serves 4

¼   cup, plus 3 tablespoons Bertolli® extra-virgin olive oil

2   tablespoons Amore®garlic paste or 6 cloves garlic, chopped

1½ pounds thin pork chops
    Salt and freshly ground pepper

2   medium Spanish (yellow) onions, sliced thin

1   tablespoon ground cumin

1   35-ounce can whole peeled plum tomatoes in puree, roughly chopped (reserve puree)

1   cup chopped fresh cilantro

Pork Burgers with Walnuts and Chow Chow

Chow chow is a pickled relish made with some combination of vegetables, gherkins, lima beans, kidney beans, and navy beans seasoned with vinegar, sugar, and salt. It's that sweet/sour/salty combination that makes it a great flavor detonator. —R

Serves 4

- 4 8-ounce ground pork patties
- 8 slices bacon
   Salt and freshly ground pepper
- ½ cup ground walnuts
- ⅓ cup cooking oil
- 2 cups Aunt Nellie's® sliced pickled Harvard beets, drained
- 1 cup sliced radishes
- 4 hearty hamburger buns
- 4 tablespoons prepared chow chow

See photo, page 76.

1. Heat a very large sauté pan over medium heat. Wrap each patty around the circumference with 2 slices of bacon. Season the patties on both sides with salt and pepper. Pour the walnuts onto a large plate. Dip each patty in the walnuts and press gently so they stick firmly to the patties.

2. Add the oil to the pan. When the oil is hot but not smoking, place the burgers into the pan. If the walnuts begin to brown or burn, remove the patties and wait until the pan cools off. Cook the patties until the walnuts are brown and the internal temperature has reached 155°F.

3. Meanwhile, mix the beets and radishes and set aside. When the patties are done, place each one on a hamburger bun and top with a tablespoon of chow chow. Serve with the beet salad.

Tools

very large sauté pan

Grocery List

Fresh

4 8-ounce ground pork patties
8 slices bacon
radishes
2 ounces walnuts

Packaged

15.5-ounce jar Aunt Nellie's®
pickled Harvard beets
4 hearty hamburger buns
17-ounce jar chow chow

Staples

cooking oil

less than 30 minutes

Pork Chops with Potatoes

One of my top 10 favorite dishes is a simple classic from the region of Campania in Italy that's made with rabbit, potatoes, and rosemary. This is a take on this dish that's made with pork instead of rabbit. —R

Tools

large sauté pan

rimmed baking pan

Grocery List

Fresh

4 pork loin chops (about 1¾ pounds)
2 green peppers
4 Idaho potatoes

Packaged

1-ounce package fresh rosemary

Staples

extra-virgin olive oil

1. Preheat the oven to 500°F.

2. Heat a large sauté pan over high heat. When it's hot, add the olive oil and heat until it just begins to smoke. While oil is heating, pat dry one side of the pork chops with a clean paper towel to prevent splattering. Season that side with salt and pepper. Place the chops, seasoned side down, in the pan and brown them, about 2 minutes. When the first side is brown, pat the side that is facing up with a paper towel and season with salt and pepper. Turn the chops over and brown them, another 2 minutes.

3. Remove the chops from the skillet and place on a rimmed baking pan. With the heat remaining on high, add the peppers and potatoes to the pan. Season with salt and pepper. Cover and cook the peppers and potatoes until they begin to soften, about 3 minutes. Add the rosemary and season to taste with salt and pepper, if necessary.

4. Add the pork chops and their juices back to the sauté pan and place the pan in the oven until pork and potatoes are cooked, about 10 to 15 minutes.

Serves 4

¼ cup Bertolli® extra-virgin olive oil

4 loin pork chops (about 1¾ pounds total)
   Salt and freshly ground pepper

2 green peppers, seeded and cut into strips

4 medium Idaho potatoes, peeled and cut into 8 wedges

2 tablespoons roughly chopped fresh rosemary

Pork Kabobs with Rosemary-Prune Glaze

I have never been good at planning ahead, but I do expect my food to taste great, so I like to use thick, highly flavored glazes instead of marinades for grilling. They stick immediately and taste even better when they char on the grill. —R

Serves 4

- ½ cup Martini & Rossi® rosso vermouth
- 3 tablespoons red wine vinegar
- 1½ cup pitted prunes
- 1 tablespoon freshly ground pepper
- 3 tablespoons chopped fresh rosemary
- 1 teaspoon Amore® garlic paste or 1 garlic clove, chopped
- 8 pork kabobs, about 1½ pounds
- 2 large red onions, peeled and sliced ½ inch thick
- Salt and freshly ground pepper

1. Heat a grill/grill pan/broiler on high.

2. In a food processor, blend vermouth, vinegar, prunes, pepper, rosemary, and garlic until mixture resembles a thick paste.

3. Brush kabobs and onions generously with the prune glaze. Season with salt and pepper. Grill kabobs and onions, rotating and turning occasionally, for about 10 minutes, or until pork is cooked throughout.

4. Serve kabobs with grilled onions.

Tools

grill pan

food processor

Grocery List

Fresh

8 pork kabobs (1½ pounds)

Packaged

750 ml bottle Martini & Rossi® rosso vermouth
24-ounce package pitted prunes
1-ounce package fresh rosemary
3.15-ounce tube Amore® garlic paste

Staples

red wine vinegar
large red onions

Pork Medallions with Shrimp & Penne Primavera

Packaged food has come a long way. I use a frozen pasta dish by Bertolli® in this recipe because it makes a great starch-and-vegetable side dish for the pork. The pasta is deliciously seasoned so there's no need for an additional sauce. –R

Tools

grill pan

large saucepan

Grocery List

Fresh

1½ pounds pork tenderloin

Packaged

24-ounce package frozen Bertolli® Mediterranean-Style™ Shrimp and Penne Primavera

Staples

red onion
Tabasco® sauce
honey

1. Preheat a grill/grill pan/broiler on high.

2. Heat a large saucepan over medium-high heat. Empty the contents of the Bertolli package in the pan. Cover and cook for 8 minutes, stirring occasionally.

3. Meanwhile, season the pork medallions on both sides with salt and pepper. In a large mixing bowl toss the pork with the onion, Tabasco®, and honey. Grill over high heat about 3 to 4 minutes per side, or until pork and onions are charred and the internal temperature of the pork is 155°F.

4. Toss the pasta and season with salt and pepper, if necessary. Serve with the grilled pork medallions.

Serves 4

1   24-ounce package frozen Bertolli® Mediterranean-Style™ Shrimp & Penne Primavera

1½ pound pork tenderloin, cut into 4 medallions and flattened with the heel of your palm

Salt and freshly ground pepper

1   cup thinly sliced red onion

1   teaspoon Tabasco® sauce

1   tablespoon honey

Pork Medallions with Apricot & Endive

Tarragon and basil are both anise flavored. Fresh basil is ubiquitous, so if you can't find fresh tarragon, use basil—or dried tarragon. Use one-fourth of the dried vs. the fresh, and rehydrate it for a few minutes in whatever liquid is in the recipe—here, in the red wine dressing. –R

Serves 4

1 cup Ken's® steak house lite red wine vinegar and olive oil dressing
2 tablespoons apricot preserves
1 tablespoon chopped fresh tarragon
1½ pounds pork tenderloin, cut into 4 medallions and flattened with the heel of your palm
Salt and freshly ground pepper
5 heads Belgian endive, cored and sliced

See photo, page 65.

1. Preheat a grill/grill pan/broiler on high.

2. In a large bowl combine the dressing, apricot preserves, and tarragon. Set aside.

3. Meanwhile, season the pork medallions with salt and pepper on both sides. Grill over high heat until the internal temperature reaches 155°F, about 3 to 4 minutes per side.

4. Add the sliced endive to the bowl with the dressing and toss to coat. Season to taste with salt and black pepper.

5. Serve medallions with a side of endive salad.

Tools

grill pan

Grocery List

Fresh

1½ pounds pork tenderloin
5 heads Belgian endive

Packaged

16-ounce bottle Ken's® steak house lite red wine vinegar and olive oil dressing
12-ounce jar apricot preserves
1-ounce package fresh tarragon

Staples

less than 15 minutes

Pork Chops with Turnip Greens, Black-Eyed Peas, and Fresh Cranberry Relish

Fresh cranberries can be hard to find other than around the holidays, so I made this cranberry relish with whole berry cranberry sauce—available any time of year in cans—sparked up with a splash of fresh lime juice.–R

Tools

grill pan

medium saucepan

Grocery List

Fresh

8 boneless thin-cut pork loin chops

Packaged

12-ounce can Ocean Spray® whole berry cranberry sauce
15-ounce can Bush's® Best turnip greens
14-ounce can Progresso® black-eyed peas

Staples

limes

1. Preheat a grill/grill pan/broiler on high.

2. Meanwhile, in a medium bowl combine the cranberry sauce, lime juice, and a pinch of salt and mix well. Set aside.

3. Season the pork chops with salt and pepper on both sides and grill them until they reach an internal temperature of 155°F, about 3 to 4 minutes per side.

4. Meanwhile, in a medium saucepan combine the turnip greens and black-eyed peas and bring to a simmer over high heat. Season to taste with salt and pepper.

5. Top each chop with a spoonful of cranberry relish. Serve chops alongside turnip greens and black-eyed peas.

Serves 4

- 1   12-ounce can Ocean Spray® whole berry cranberry sauce
     Juice of 2 limes
     Salt and freshly ground pepper
- 8   boneless thin-cut pork loin chops
- 1   15-ounce can Bush's® Best turnip greens, drained
- 1   14-ounce can Progresso® black-eyed peas, drained

Crispy **Pork Chops** with Rice & Beans

less than 30 minutes

Minute® Rice is really good, especially if you flavor it with Cajun seasoning and combine it with a classic partner like black beans. Most nights, I'm too time constrained to wait for rice to cook—and I'm always impatient to eat when there's fried pork on the table. –R

Serves 4

2 cups chicken broth
1½ teaspoons Cajun seasoning
1 cup Premium Minute® rice
1 15-ounce can Progresso® black beans, rinsed and drained
1 cup Bertolli® extra-virgin olive oil
1 cup all-purpose flour
Salt and freshly ground pepper
8 2½-ounce thin pork loin chops
2 whole limes, cut in half
2 cups whole cilantro sprigs, washed

1. In a medium saucepan bring the chicken broth and 1 teaspoon of the Cajun seasoning to a boil. Add the rice, cover, and turn heat down to low. Simmer for 5 minutes. Add the drained beans to the rice. Cover and let sit for 5 minutes.

2. Meanwhile, heat a large sauté pan over high. Add the olive oil and let it get hot.

3. In a shallow dish, season the flour with remaining ½ teaspoon Cajun seasoning, along with salt and pepper to taste. Season the pork chops generously with salt and pepper and toss in the flour.

4. When the oil becomes slightly smoky, add the chops to the pan. Cook until crispy and golden brown, about 4 minutes per side for medium doneness. Remove the chops to a paper towel-lined plate to drain. Season with salt and pepper to taste, if necessary.

5. Plate up the pork chops with the rice and beans and squeeze the juice of half a lime over each dish.

6. Top with the cilantro sprigs and serve.

Tools

medium saucepan

large sauté pan

Grocery List

Fresh

8 2½-ounce thin pork loin chops
1 bunch cilantro

Packaged

2.3-ounce bottle Cajun seasoning
14-ounce box Premium Minute® rice
15-ounce can Progresso® black beans

Staples

chicken broth
extra-virgin olive oil
flour/limes

Sausage, Peppers & Tomatoes
with Fennel Seeds

I can't verify that sausage and peppers is an authentic Italian dish. I'm guessing Italian-American immigrants invented it in the nineteenth century. My mom made it for big events. In New York it was the star of every street fair, right behind zeppole. —R

Tools

small skillet

large sauté pan

Grocery List

Fresh

1 pound sweet Italian link sausage
1 pound spicy Italian link sausage
3 green peppers

Packaged

3.15-ounce tube Amore® garlic paste
1750 ml bottle dry red wine
4-ounce can diced tomatoes with Italian herbs

Staples

fennel seeds
extra-virgin olive oil
tomato paste/ pasta

1. In a small skillet, toast fennel seeds over medium heat, stirring frequently, until lightly browned and fragrant, about 5 to 7 minutes. Set aside.

2. Heat a large sauté pan over high heat. Add the olive oil and let it get hot. Gently place the sausages in the pan and brown them on all sides, covered, about 3 minutes.

3. Add the peppers and cook, stirring occasionally, until they begin to soften. Add the garlic and toasted fennel seeds and cook, stirring, until fragrant, about 1 minute. Add the wine, tomatoes, and tomato paste. Lower the heat and simmer, partially covered, for 10 to 15 minutes until sausages are fully cooked.

4. Remove the sausages from the pan. Cool slightly and slice into 1-inch-thick pieces. Return to the sauce and heat through. Serve on hot cooked pasta or with Italian bread, if desired.

Serves 4

1 tablespoon fennel seeds
3 tablespoons Bertolli® extra-virgin olive oil
1 pound sweet Italian link sausage
1 pound package spicy Italian link sausage
3 green peppers, cut into ½-inch-wide strips
1 tablespoon Amore® garlic paste or 3 garlic cloves, chopped
2 cups dry red wine
1 14-ounce can diced tomatoes with Italian herbs
1 6-ounce can tomato paste
½ pound dried pasta, cooked according to package instructions, or Italian-style bread (optional)

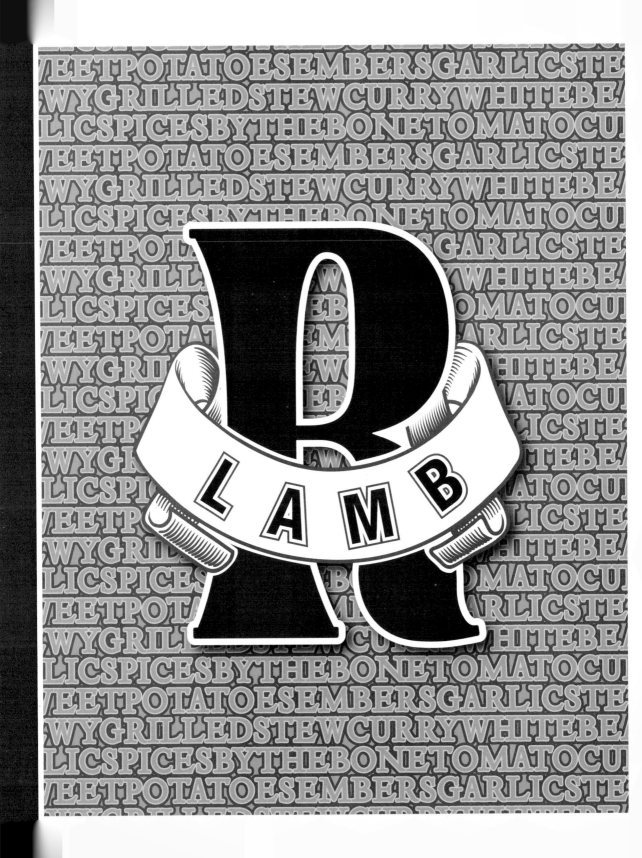

"Cooking is the nicest thing you can do for a person. When a child is born, the first thing a mother does is feed it."

Caramelized **Lamb Chops**
with Carrot & Mushroom Stew

In 1987 I worked in Paris for a chef named Dominique Cecillon. He took great care of me. He also taught me a lot. One dish that struck me was an old recipe called *barigoule*, which refers to anything cooked with mushrooms and bacon. This is my version. –R

Tools

Large saucepan

large sauté pan

Grocery List

Fresh

12 lamb chops (about 2 pounds)
12 slices bacon
2 cups whole white mushrooms

Packaged

2 16-ounce packages baby carrots
1-ounce package fresh thyme
3.15-ounce tube Amore® garlic paste

Staples

chicken broth
extra-virgin olive oil
red wine vinegar

1. In a large saucepan, combine the chicken broth, carrots, and thyme. Season to taste with salt and pepper and bring it to a boil. Cover, reduce to a simmer, and cook until carrots are soft, about 15 minutes.

2. Meanwhile, heat a large sauté pan over high heat. Add the olive oil to the pan. When the oil is hot, pat the lamb chops dry with a paper towel and season both sides generously with salt and pepper. Place half of the chops in the pan and cook without moving the meat until light brown, about 1 minute. Turn the chops over and continue to cook until light brown, about 1 minute more. Remove chops from the pan and put them on a platter. Repeat with remaining chops. When they are all cooked, let the chops rest at room temperature or put them in a warm oven (200°F).

3. In the same pan over medium heat, cook the bacon just until most of the fat has been rendered. It should be soft, not crispy; adjust the heat if necessary. Add the garlic and mushrooms, cover, and cook for 2 minutes. Add the vinegar and cook, uncovered, until the liquid has reduced by a third. Add all of the carrots and half of the seasoned broth to the sauté pan and bring to a simmer. Cook until the liquid has reduced by about a third and is no longer soupy. Season to taste with salt and pepper.

4. Divide the lamb chops (three per person) among four large soup plates. Spoon a generous amount of the carrot and mushroom stew over the top and serve.

Serves 4

3   14-ounce cans chicken broth
2   16-ounce packages peeled baby carrots
½   bunch fresh thyme
    Salt and freshly ground pepper
4   tablespoons Bertolli® extra-virgin olive oil
12 lamb chops (about 2 pounds)
12 slices bacon, cut crosswise into 1-inch pieces
6   tablespoons Amore® garlic paste or 18 garlic cloves, chopped
2   cups whole white mushrooms
¼   cup red wine vinegar

Curried **Grilled Lamb Chops** with Chicory

less than 15 minutes

Curry powder is one of the greatest inventions of all time. Our job as cooks is to create great taste by combining ingredients—and with curry powder it's all done for you! It goes with everything and even a teaspoon gets you very far down the road to great flavor. –R

Serves 4

- 2 cups Fage® Greek yogurt or whole-milk plain yogurt
- 4 teaspoons Amore® garlic paste or 4 garlic cloves, chopped
- 1½ tablespoon honey
- 2 tablespoons curry powder
- 4 tablespoons Bertolli® extra-virgin olive oil
- 12 2- to 2½-ounce lamb chops
  Salt and freshly ground pepper
- 2 large bunches chicory, roughly chopped
- ⅓ cup chopped fresh cilantro

1. Preheat a grill/grill pan/broiler on high.

2. In a medium bowl, combine the yogurt, garlic, honey, curry powder, and 2 tablespoons of the olive oil. Set aside a third of the yogurt mixture. Completely coat the lamb chops with the remaining yogurt mixture. Season chops generously with salt and pepper.

3. Grill the chops on high heat until medium or medium rare, about 2 minutes per side.

4. Meanwhile, heat 2 large sauté pans over high heat with 1 tablespoon of olive oil in each pan. Add half of the chopped chicory to each pan. Season chicory lightly with salt and pepper. Cook, stirring occasionally, until wilted and tender, about 2 minutes.

5. Place the wilted greens in a colander and press down on them with the back of a large spoon to release extra liquid; transfer to a large bowl.

6. Toss the warm chicory with the cilantro and the reserved yogurt mixture. Season to taste with salt and pepper and serve with lamb chops.

Tools

grill pan

2 large sauté pans

Grocery List

Fresh

12 2- to 2½-ounce lamb chops
2 large bunches chicory
1 bunch cilantro

Packaged

16-ounce container Fage®
Greek yogurt
3.15-ounce tube Amore® garlic
paste

Staples

honey
curry powder
extra-virgin olive oil

Grilled Baby Lamb Chops
& Heirloom Tomatoes

I can eat grilled lamb all summer—as an appetizer, passed hors d'oeuvre, or entrée. I even love cold leftover roast lamb as a snack or as a savory breakfast with yogurt. Lamb is best when it's combined with something acidic—in this case, tomatoes. —R

1. Preheat a grill/grill pan/broiler on high.

2. Set aside a fourth of the parsley and chop it fine for a garnish. Refrigerate it until ready to serve. Roughly chop the remaining parsley and oregano and transfer to a medium bowl. Add the lemon juice, olive oil, peppercorns, and bay leaf halves. Whisk well to combine.

3. Put the lamb chops in a shallow dish and coat with half of the marinade. Refrigerate for at least one hour.

4. Cut tomatoes into thick slices and put in a shallow dish. Cover with the remaining marinade, turning slices to coat well. Let sit at room temperature.

5. Remove the lamb and the tomatoes from the marinade and season generously with salt and pepper. Grill the lamb until medium, about 3 to 4 minutes per side.

6. When the meat is just about done, place the tomatoes on the grill and cook until they are warmed through and slightly wilted, turning once.

7. Remove the tomatoes from the grill and arrange on a platter. Top with the lamb chops, sprinkle with the finely chopped fresh parsley, and serve immediately.

Serves 4

- 1 bunch fresh flat-leaf parsley, leaves only
- 5 sprigs oregano, leaves only
- 4 tablespoons fresh lemon juice
- 1½ cups Bertolli® extra-virgin olive oil
- 3 black peppercorns, crushed
- 1 bay leaf, torn in half
- 12 baby lamb chops
- 6 large heirloom tomatoes, like Brandywine, German Stripe, Persimmon, or 12 medium-sized tomatoes, cored

  Salt and freshly ground pepper

Grilled Lamb with Sweet and Sour Eggplant

My **Aunt** Margaret used to make *caponata*, a Sicilian sweet-and-sour eggplant condiment. She was a great cook—and this was one of her best dishes. You can add capers, pine nuts, and raisins, if you like. Just keep it sweet and sour, and it goes great with lamb chops. –R

Serves 4

½ cup Bertolli® extra-virgin olive oil, plus more for drizzling
1 large red onion, cut into large dice
3 tablespoons Amore® garlic paste or 6 large cloves garlic, chopped
1 large eggplant, cut into ¾-inch cubes (about 1½ pounds)
   Salt and freshly ground pepper
1 14-ounce can whole peeled plum tomatoes in puree
⅔ cup chopped olives, preferably pitted, Mediterranean medley
2 tablespoons red wine vinegar
1½ tablespoons sugar
12 2-ounce lamb chops

1. Preheat a grill/grill pan/broiler pan on high.

2. In a very large sauté pan, heat ⅓ cup of the olive oil over medium-high heat. Add the onion and about two-thirds of the chopped garlic and sauté for 1 minute. Add the eggplant. Season generously with salt and pepper and cook, stirring often, until eggplant is tender, about 8 minutes. Add the tomatoes to the pan, crushing them lightly with your hands as you add them. Pour in any remaining tomato puree. Cook mixture over medium-high heat, stirring occasionally, until most of the liquid has evaporated.

3. Stir in the chopped olives, vinegar, and sugar. Season to taste with salt and pepper and remove from the heat.*

4. While the caponata is cooking, mix the remaining chopped garlic with the remaining olive oil. Coat the lamb chops with this mixture. Season the chops generously with salt and pepper and place on the grill. Cook until chops are medium, about 2½ minutes per side. Remove from the grill and let rest for 5 minutes.

5. Drizzle the caponata with a little bit of olive oil and serve with the lamb chops.

✱ Caponata is best served at room temperature.

Tools

very large sauté pan

grill pan

Grocery List

Fresh

1 large eggplant
12 lamb chops (about 2 ounces each)

Packaged

3.15-ounce tube Amore® garlic paste
14-ounce can whole peeled plum tomatoes in puree
12-ounce jar Mediterranean olive medley

Staples

extra-virgin olive oil
red onion/red wine
vinegar/sugar

Lamb Chops with Tiny White Beans & Raisins

Raisins and pine nuts are the dynamic duo of southern Mediterranean cooking. You'll find them in Sicilian meatballs and in a dish called kufta all over the Middle East. The raisin condiment is a great accompaniment to roasted meats and grilled fish. –R

Tools

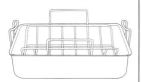

large roasting pan

large saucepan

Grocery List

Fresh

3 to 4 pounds baby lamb racks

Packaged

15-ounce package Sun-Maid® golden raisins
2 14-ounce cans Progresso® cannellini beans
1-ounce package fresh mint
3-ounce package pine nuts

Staples

chicken broth
extra-virgin olive oil
red wine vinegar

1. Remove lamb from the refrigerator 30 minutes before cooking. Preheat oven to 400°F.

2. Brush the lamb with the olive oil and then season generously all over with salt and pepper. Put in a large roasting pan and then in the oven on the lowest shelf. Roast for about 15 minutes if you like your lamb a little pink inside—a few minutes more for well done (especially if each rack weighs about 2 pounds). Remove from the oven and let rest for 10 minutes.

3. Meanwhile, heat a large saucepan over medium heat. Add raisins, chicken broth, and vinegar and bring to a boil. Cook for 5 minutes. Add the beans and simmer until mixture resembles a juicy stew, about 3 to 5 minutes. Add the mint and turn off the heat. Season to taste with salt and pepper.

4. To serve, cut the lamb into 4 portions, if necessary. Divide the bean-raisin mixture evenly among four plates. Top with a fourth of the lamb. Sprinkle with toasted pine nuts, season to taste with salt and pepper, and serve.

✳ To toast pine nuts, put them in a small skillet over medium heat, stirring frequently, until light golden brown, about 6 to 8 minutes.

Serves 4

3   to 4 pounds baby lamb racks (the smaller the better—ideally a ¾- to 1-pound New Zealand lamb rack per person), completely trimmed of any fat and sinew

¼   cup Bertolli® extra-virgin olive oil

    Salt and freshly ground pepper

¼   cup Sun-Maid® golden raisins

¼   cup canned chicken broth

¼   cup red wine vinegar

2   14-ounce cans Progresso® cannellini beans, rinsed and drained

1   bunch fresh mint, chopped

½   cup pine nuts, toasted*

Loin Lamb Chops alla Pizzaiolo

The *pizzaiolo* is the pizza man. When I worked in pizzerias, the guy who flipped the dough was a rock star. In Italy they named a dish after him, so naturally there's tomato sauce involved. *Steak alla pizzaiolo* was my birthday dish as a kid. –R

Serves 4

- 3 tablespoons Bertolli® extra-virgin olive oil
- 8 lamb loin chops, about 2½ inches thick (about 1¾ pounds total)
  Salt and freshly ground pepper
- 1 onion, sliced
- 2 medium Idaho potatoes, peeled and cut into half moons (about ¼ inch thick)
- 1 12-ounce jar Mancini® roasted peppers, sliced
- 1 cup red wine
- 1 25-ounce jar Victoria® marinara sauce
- 2 tablespoons finely chopped fresh rosemary
- ¼ cup chopped fresh flat-leaf parsley

1. In a large sauté pan, heat the olive oil over high heat. Season the lamb chops generously with salt and pepper and lay them in the pan. Cook until deep golden brown, about 3 minutes per side. Remove from pan and set aside.

2. Turn the heat to medium and add the onion and potatoes to the pan; season with salt and pepper. Gently cook, but don't brown, the vegetables until they start to become tender, about 5 minutes. Add the peppers, wine, and marinara; bring the mixture to a boil. Sprinkle the sauce with rosemary, cover, and turn heat down to a simmer. Cook for about 20 minutes, or until the potatoes are tender. Season to taste with salt and pepper, if necessary.

3. Add the lamb chops and their juices back to the pan just until heated through, about 3 minutes.

4. Sprinkle the parsley on top and serve.

Tools

large sauté pan

Grocery List

Fresh

8 lamb loin chops (about 1¾ pounds)
2 medium Idaho potatoes
1 bunch flat-leaf parsley

Packaged

12-ounce jar Mancini® roasted peppers
25-ounce jar Victoria® marinara sauce
1-ounce package fresh rosemary

Staples

onion
red wine
extra-virgin olive oil

less than 30 minutes

Quick **Lamb Stew** with Sweet Red Wine Sauce

In Italy there is a dish called *brodetto*, which means little broth. Here we'd call it a fricassee. It's really just a quick stew made with a small amount of liquid. When I cook lamb I always incorporate something acidic like wine, vinegar, or lemon juice. –R

Tools

large sauté pan

Grocery List

Fresh

2 pounds boneless lamb stew meat
1 green Cubanelle pepper

Packaged

12-ounce jar Patak's® hot mango chutney
15-ounce jar Aunt Nellie's® Harvard beets

Staples

extra-virgin olive oil
red onions
dry red wine

1. Heat a large sauté pan over high heat. When the pan is hot, add the oil to the pan.

2. When the oil is shimmering and slightly smoky, season the lamb with salt and pepper and carefully lay half of it in the pan. Brown the meat evenly on all sides. Remove the meat from the pan and set aside. Repeat with remaining lamb.

3. Carefully add the onions and pepper to the pan. Cook, stirring occasionally, for about 3 to 4 minutes. Add the red wine, stirring and scraping up any flavorful bits that are stuck to the pan. Add the chutney and simmer on medium heat for 5 minutes.

4. Add the lamb back to the pan, along with the beets. Let simmer just until everything is heated through, about 1 minute.

Serves 4

5	tablespoons Bertolli® extra-virgin olive oil
2	pounds boneless lamb stew meat, cut into bite-size pieces

Salt and freshly ground pepper

4	red onions, peeled and cut into large chunks
1	green Cubanelle pepper, cut into large chunks
2	cups good-quality dry red wine
1	12-ounce jar Patak's® hot mango chutney
1	15-ounce jar Aunt Nellie's® Harvard beets

Open-Faced **Lamb Sandwich**
with Cucumber Raita

I love lamb sandwiches—and if you've ever eaten a gyro, you do too. Here the tartness of the lemon and yogurt balance the heady richness of the lamb—and the cucumber and watercress provide a satisfying crunch. –R

Serves 4

- 1 pound top round lamb, cut into 1-inch-thick medallions
- 2 tablespoons Bertolli® extra-virgin olive oil
  Salt and freshly ground pepper
- 1 large seedless cucumber, peeled and cut into half moons (about 2 cups)
- 1 cup Fage® Greek yogurt
  Zest and juice of 1 lemon
- ⅓ cup chopped fresh mint
- 1 small bunch watercress or ¼ pound of arugula
- 4 large slices rustic sourdough bread, toasted

See photo, page 74.

1. Preheat a grill/grill pan/broiler on high.

2. Coat the lamb with a little bit of the olive oil and season both sides with salt and pepper. Cook the lamb until medium rare, about 4 minutes per side. Let rest for about 10 minutes.*

3. Meanwhile, place the cucumber in a medium bowl and microwave for about 2 minutes or until cucumber is cooked but still has texture. Drain any liquid from the cucumber. Mix cucumber with the yogurt, lemon zest, and mint. Season to taste with salt and pepper.

4. In a separate bowl, toss the watercress with the lemon juice and remaining olive oil; season to taste with salt and pepper. Slice the lamb as thin as possible with a very sharp knife.

5. To assemble the sandwiches, top the bread with some of the cucumber mixture. Top the cucumber with the lamb slices. Finally, mound some watercress salad on top of the lamb and serve immediately.

✳ Refrigerate the lamb overnight if you can. That will make it the perfect texture for a sandwich and easy to slice. Leftover roast leg of lamb also works great.

Tool

grill pan

Grocery List

Fresh

1 pound top round lamb
1 large seedless cucumber
1 bunch watercress

Packaged

2 7-ounce containers Fage® Greek yogurt
1-ounce package fresh mint
1 loaf rustic sourdough bread

Staples

extra-virgin olive oil
lemon

less than 15 minutes

Cinnamon-Rubbed **Grilled Lamb Chops** with Sweet Potatoes

The quality of shortcut foods is great these days. For instance, since sweet potatoes take about an hour to cook from scratch, I'm always looking for a better way. This packaged product is very good. The potatoes aren't too sweet and are cooked just right. –R

Tools

grill pan

medium microwaveable bowl

Grocery List

Fresh

12 lamb chops

Packaged

16-ounce package Diner's Choice® mashed sweet potatoes
1-ounce package fresh basil

Staples

garlic
cinnamon

1. Preheat a grill/grill pan/broiler on high.

2. In a small bowl combine garlic and olive oil. Rub lamb chops all over with it. Season chops generously with salt. In another small bowl combine the cinnamon and pepper. Coat both sides of each chop with the spice mixture.

3. Place the lamb chops on the grill. Cook for 3½ to 4 minutes per side for medium rare to medium.

4. Meanwhile, heat the mashed sweet potatoes in the microwave until hot, about 4 minutes, stirring twice. Season potatoes to taste with more salt, if necessary. Drizzle potatoes with olive oil and stir in the basil.

5. Serve the lamb chops on a bed of the mashed sweet potatoes.

Serves 4

5   garlic cloves, chopped
4   tablespoon Bertolli® extra-virgin olive oil, plus more for drizzling
12 lamb chops
    Salt
1   teaspoon ground cinnamon
1   tablespoon freshly ground black pepper
1   16-ounce package Diner's Choice® mashed sweet potatoes
½   cup fresh basil, chopped

See photo, page 75.

SALMON

"Recipes are merely a starting point. Once you get cooking, make it your own—discover your own culinary destiny. "

Salmon with Crunchy Broccoli & Lemon Butter

I like to poach fish in something other than water because it tastes better and makes a great sauce when you're done poaching. I use lemon butter here because salmon needs a rich cooking liquid to keep it from drying out. —R

Tools

very large saucepan

broiler pan

Grocery List

Fresh

4 8-ounce boneless, skinless salmon fillets
2 bunches broccoli

Packaged

1-ounce package fresh tarragon

Staples

butter
lemons

1. Heat a very large saucepan over medium-high heat. Add the butter to the pan. When butter is just melted, remove 2 tablespoons and set aside. Continue to cook the butter until it's a deep brown color, swirling often. Remove the pan from heat and add the lemon juice. Continue swirling to blend and make a smooth sauce.

2. Lay the salmon in the sauce. Cover and simmer gently over medium heat until salmon is just cooked through, about 7 to 8 minutes. Season to taste with salt and pepper; keep warm.

3. While salmon is poaching prepare the broccoli.

4. Heat a broiler on high. In a large bowl toss the broccoli with the reserved melted butter. Place the broccoli on a foil-covered broiler pan and broil it until golden brown, about 3 to 4 minutes.

5. Toss the crunchy broccoli with the lemon zest and tarragon. Arrange on a platter. Spoon about two-thirds of the lemon sauce evenly over the vegetables. Lay the salmon on top of the broccoli and spoon the remaining sauce over the fish.

Serves 4

1½ sticks butter
   Juice and zest of 3 lemons
4   8-ounce boneless, skinless salmon fillets
   Salt and freshly ground pepper
5   cups of broccoli florets, washed and dried
3   tablespoons chopped fresh tarragon

Curried **Salmon** with Beet Tartar Salad

less than 15 minutes

Beets, curry, tartar sauce? The ravings of a lunatic? Taste it before you judge. This dish is a perfect example of how experimentation can make you an artist in the kitchen. I call it a salad instead of a sauce because the ingredients aren't chopped or pureed. —R

Serves 4

- ⅓ cup drained pickled beets
- ⅓ cup drained cocktail onions
- ¼ cup B&G® hot dog relish
- ¾ cup mayonnaise
- 2 tablespoons lemon juice
  Salt and freshly ground pepper
- ¼ cup Bertolli® extra-virgin olive oil
- 3 tablespoons curry powder
- 4 8-ounce boneless, skinless salmon fillets

1. Heat a grill/grill pan/broiler on high.

2. In a medium bowl mix together the beets, onions, relish, mayonnaise, and lemon juice until combined. Season the salad to taste with salt and pepper. Cover and chill until serving time.

3. In a shallow dish combine the olive oil with curry powder and salt and pepper to taste. Toss the fish in the seasoned oil.

4. Place the salmon on the grill and cook until fish is golden brown and cooked through, about 3 minutes per side.

5. Serve salmon with the chilled tartar salad.

Tools

grill pan

Grocery List

Fresh

4 8-ounce boneless, skinless salmon fillets

Packaged

16-ounce jar sliced pickled beets
3.5-ounce jar cocktail onions
10-ounce jar B&G® hot dog relish

Staples

mayonnaise/lemon juice
extra-virgin olive oil
curry powder

less than 15
minutes

Salmon with Lima Beans & Basil

Patak's is a maker of Indian condiments such as sauces, pickles, and other great-tasting concoctions. Adding one teaspoon of any of this complex and fabulous stuff is like adding 20 new ingredients. The lima beans taste like they were reincarnated as higher beings. —R

Tools

broiler pan

large sauté pan

Grocery List

Fresh

4 10-ounce salmon steaks
1 baguette

Packaged

12-ounce jar Patak's® hot mango chutney
10-ounce package frozen lima beans
1-ounce package fresh basil

Staples

chicken broth
lemons

1. Preheat broiler to 550°F.

2. Lay the salmon on a baking sheet or broiler pan. Season with salt and pepper. Broil, turning once, until salmon is just cooked through, about 8 to 10 minutes.

3. In a large dry sauté pan, toast the bread over medium-high heat for about 3 to 4 minutes, turning the pieces on all sides.

4. Leave the bread in the pan and add the chutney and the chicken broth. Let the liquid bubble up, then add the lima beans, lemon juice, and half of the lemon zest. Cook until the lima beans are tender, about 3 to 5 minutes.

5. Divide the bread-and-bean mixture among four plates and add a salmon steak to each. Garnish with remaining lemon zest and torn fresh basil and serve.

Serves 4

4	10-ounce salmon steaks
	Salt and freshly ground pepper
½	baguette, ripped into small chunks
1	cup Patak's® hot mango chutney
1	cup chicken broth
1½	cups frozen lima beans
	Juice and zest of 2 lemons
½	bunch basil leaves, torn

Tea-Smoked **Salmon Fillet**
with Sweet & Sour Potato Salad

less than 30
minutes

Smoking isn't the long, arduous process everyone thinks it is. This is a quick and very hot smoke method that cooks while it smokes. The trick is to use tender cuts that don't need to be cooked forever. Everyone has tea in the cupboard, and it's very aromatic. —R

Serves 4

1 cup Aunt Nellie's® pickled beets, drained
1 cup Aunt Nellie's® pickled onions, drained and cut into small chunks
½ bunch scallions, sliced thin
2 pounds of your favorite potato salad
  Salt and freshly ground pepper
4 6-ounce boneless, skinless salmon fillets
2 10×12×3-inch disposable aluminum pans
1 10×10 cooling or all-purpose roasting rack

For the tea-smoking mixture:
½ cup orange pekoe, Darjeeling, or your favorite aromatic tea leaves
½ cup rice

1. Preheat the oven to 400°F, or heat a grill on medium high.

2. In a large microwaveable bowl toss the beets, onions, and scallions. Gently fold in the potato salad. Season lightly with salt and pepper. Microwave on high for 2 minutes.

3. Mix the tea-smoking mixture thoroughly and place in one of the aluminum pans. Place the rack over the top of the pan so that it is suspended. Put the pan on the stove top over medium to high heat and allow mixture to start to smoke.

4. Season the salmon fillets generously with salt and pepper. Place on the rack above the smoking mixture. Turn the other aluminum pan upside down and cover the salmon so that the smoke is contained.

5. At this point you can continue smoking the fish on top of the stove, or you can place the pans in the oven for 7 to 8 minutes, or until salmon is just cooked through. (If you're using the grill, close the lid and cook for about 9 to 12 minutes.)

6. Serve salmon alongside the potato salad.

Tools

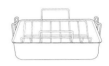

large microwaveable bowl

roasting rack

Grocery List

Fresh

4 6-ounce boneless, skinless salmon fillets
1 bunch scallions

Packaged

16-ounce Aunt Nellie's® pickled beets
15-ounce Aunt Nellie's® pickled onions
2 pounds potato salad
½ cup orange pekoe tea leaves

Staples

rice

Miso Marmalade **Salmon** with Swiss Chard

The combination of orange marmalade and miso paste might very well be my favorite creation. I've used it as a glaze on duck, pork, and of course, fish. It lasts forever and when it browns, it transforms into something magical. –R

Tools

broiler pan

large sauté pan

Grocery List

Fresh

2 bunches Swiss chard
4 8-ounce boneless, skinless salmon fillets

Packaged

6-ounce container miso paste
12-ounce container orange marmalade

Staples

extra-virgin olive oil

1. Preheat broiler on high.

2. Heat a large sauté pan on high. Add ¼ cup of the oil to the hot pan. When oil is shimmering and almost smoking, add the Swiss chard and season lightly with salt and pepper. Cover and turn the heat down to medium. Cook, stirring often, until tender, about 5 to 7 minutes.

3. Meanwhile mix the miso paste, marmalade, and water in a small bowl. Using a pastry brush, thoroughly paint the miso mixture over the salmon. Season with pepper only.

4. Brush the broiler pan with the remaining 1 tablespoon of oil. Lay the salmon on the pan and broil until the miso coating is charred and bubbling, about 5 to 6 minutes. The salmon should be just cooked through.

5. Serve the salmon on a bed of the Swiss chard.

tip You may also use a 27-ounce can of Glory Foods® seasoned southern-style greens, your choice of turnip, collard, or mixed.

Serves 4

⅓ cup Bertolli® extra-virgin olive oil

24 ounces chopped Swiss chard (2 12-ounce packages of prewashed and cut, or 2 whole bunches, washed and cut)*

½ cup miso paste

½ cup orange marmalade

2 tablespoons water

4 8-ounce boneless, skinless salmon fillets

  Salt and freshly ground pepper

Sautéed **Summer Roll of Salmon**
with Basil Pesto

less than 30 minutes

A **summer** roll is just like a spring roll but not cooked. Spring rolls are deep-fried. This roll is sautéed, so it's somewhere in between. The result is fresh and light like a summer roll but pleasantly crispy—and not greasy and heavy like a spring roll. –R

Serves 4

- 2 tablespoons Bertolli® extra-virgin olive oil
- 2 tablespoons chopped fresh basil, plus 4 whole fresh basil leaves
- 1 tablespoon Amore® garlic paste or 3 cloves garlic, chopped
- 1 tablespoon chopped fresh ginger (or 1 tablespoon prepared minced ginger)
- 1 tablespoon honey
  Juice of ¼ lemon
  Salt and freshly ground pepper
- 8 large rice papers (plus a few extra in case they tear)
- 4 6-ounce salmon fillets
- 2 tablespoons butter

See photos, pages 188-189.

1. To make the pesto combine the olive oil, chopped basil, garlic, ginger, honey, and lemon juice. Season to taste with salt and pepper.

2. In a large saucepan heat 2 quarts of water to almost boiling. On a large work surface lay out a very large clean kitchen towel. Carefully—and in small increments—pour the water on the towel until almost completely soaked, allowing the water to be absorbed between additions.

3. Lay out each rice paper on one half of the towel with at least 1 inch between them on all sides. Fold the empty half over the rice paper.

4. Allow the papers to rehydrate for about 1 minute or until pliable. Working quickly, season salmon with salt and pepper. Place one whole basil leaf on top of fillet. Place fillet in the center of one wrapper. Fold in the sides. Place package, folded side down, in the center of another wrapper. Fold in the sides and place under warm towels . (If the papers soak up too much water, they'll fall apart; squeeze a little water out of the towel and try again.) Repeat for remaining fillets.

5. Heat a large skillet over medium heat. Add the butter to the pan. Before butter is completely melted place the salmon rolls in the pan, folded side down.

6. Cook until rolls are golden brown, about 2 minutes. Carefully flip them over. Cook for another 2 minutes, or until both sides are brown and crispy and salmon is cooked.

7. Remove salmon rolls from pan and top with basil pesto.

Tools

large saucepan

large skillet

Grocery List

Fresh

4 6-ounce salmon fillets

Packaged

1-ounce package fresh basil
3.15-ounce tube Amore® garlic paste
3-inch piece of ginger
16-ounce package rice paper

Staples

extra-virgin olive oil
butter/honey
lemon

Salmon Cooked in Salt with Sweet & Sour Endive

Just for giggles I included this salt dough recipe. When people see "salt crust" they are fascinated—and confused. You'd think it would make the food inedibly salty but it doesn't. In fact, sealing in any protein is the best way to guarantee *extremely* moist meat. –R

Tools

9x13-inch baking dish

very large skillet

Grocery List

Fresh

4 6-ounce skinless salmon fillets
6 heads Belgian endive

Packaged

26.5-ounce container sea salt
2-ounce jar ground turmeric
1-ounce package fresh tarragon

Staples

extra-virgin olive oil
sugar/lemons

1. Preheat the oven to 375°F.

2. In a medium bowl mix together the sea salt, turmeric, and water. It will resemble wet sand.

3. Line a 9x13-inch baking dish with aluminum foil. Cut 2 pieces of waxed paper to fit inside the baking dish. Fold each piece of waxed paper in half 3 times. With scissors cut out small holes in the waxed paper. Unfold paper.

4. Spread one cup of the sea salt mixture on the bottom of the pan. Place one piece of waxed paper on the salt. Put 1½ tablespoons olive oil in a shallow dish and dip each piece of salmon on both sides to completely coat the fillets. Season both sides of fillets with pepper. Arrange the fillets on the paper. Place the second piece of waxed paper on top of the salmon. Encase the salmon with the remaining 2 cups of salt. Put the salmon in the oven and bake for 10 to 12 minutes.

5. Meanwhile heat a very large skillet over high heat. When the skillet is hot add the remaining 2 tablespoons olive oil. When the oil is very hot (oil is smoking) add the endive. Season with salt and pepper and sauté until the endive is dark brown but not burned, about 7 to 10 minutes. Lower heat to medium and sprinkle endive with sugar and lemon juice. Cook, stirring, until endive is soft. Stir in the tarragon .

6. When the salmon reaches 120°F remove the pan from the oven. Carefully grab the paper on both sides and lift it out of the pan with all the salt in it onto a large platter. Lift out the fillets with a spatula and wipe off excess salt. Serve the salmon with the endive.

Serves 4

- 3 cups coarse sea salt
- ¼ cup ground turmeric
- ½ cup of water
  Aluminum foil
  Waxed paper
- 3½ tablespoons Bertolli® extra-virgin olive oil
- 4 6-ounce skinless salmon fillets, preferably thick center cuts
  Freshly ground pepper
- 6 heads Belgian endive, cored and sliced in large pieces
- 3 tablespoons sugar
- 3 tablespoons lemon juice
- 1 tablespoon fresh tarragon, chopped

Steamed Salmon in Napa Cabbage

less than 15 minutes

When you steam food, both nutrients and flavor are preserved. I actually prefer not to use steamers, bamboo baskets, and the like. Who needs all the extra cookware? Any time you cook a piece of meat or fish in foil (or cabbage leaves), you're steaming. —R

Serves 4

- 8 large Napa cabbage leaves
- 4 tablespoons Bertolli® extra-virgin olive oil
  Salt and freshly ground pepper
- 4 6-ounce salmon fillets
- 4 teaspoons Amoré sun-dried tomato paste
- 8 teaspoons mango or peach salsa

1. Preheat oven to 375°F.

2. Wash the cabbage leaves, drain, and lay four of them flat in a 9x13-inch baking dish. Brush the leaves lightly with olive oil and season with a little salt and pepper. Lay one salmon fillet on each leaf. Season salmon with salt and pepper. Spread 1 teaspoon of the tomato paste and 2 teaspoons of the salsa over each piece of salmon.

3. Cover each piece of salmon as tightly as possible with the remaining cabbage leaves. Put a little water in the bottom of the baking dish and cover tightly with aluminum foil.

4. Place dish in the oven and steam for about 8 minutes, or until salmon is just cooked through.

Tools

9×13-inch baking dish

Grocery List

Fresh

1 head Napa cabbage
4 6-ounce salmon fillets

Packaged

2.8-ounce tube Amore®sun-dried tomato paste
16-ounce jar mango or peach salsa

Staples

extra-virgin olive oil

Thai **Salmon Saté**

Some people think the word *saté* comes from the word satiate. Others say it means "triple stacked" in Chinese. In Asia it's a very popular street food, and every stall has a different recipe. This Thai-style recipe turns a street snack into a light, crisp entree salad. –R

Tools

grill pan

1. Preheat a grill/grill pan/broiler on high.

2. In a medium bowl, mix together sugar, lime juice, and peanut oil. Add the cucumbers, tomatoes, scallions, and cilantro and toss to combine. Season to taste with salt and pepper. Let the salad marinate while preparing the fish.

3. Evenly coat the salmon with a thin layer of the saté sauce. Season the fillets with salt and pepper. Grill until salmon is still slightly pink in the middle, about 3 minutes per side.

4. Serve the cucumber salad alongside the grilled salmon.

Serves 4

1	tablespoon sugar
	Juice of 2 limes
3	tablespoons peanut oil
2	medium cucumbers, cut in half lengthwise and sliced into half moons (about 3 cups)
2	medium tomatoes, cut into large dice
l	bunch scallions, thinly cut on a diagonal
½	cup fresh cilantro, chopped
	Salt and freshly ground pepper
4	8-ounce salmon fillets, each about 1½ inches thick
1½	cups Thai Kitchen® saté sauce, or a good peanut sauce

Grocery List

Fresh

2 medium cucumbers
2 medium tomatoes
1 bunch scallions
1 bunch cilantro
4 8-ounce salmon fillets

Packaged

13.4 ounce-bottle peanut sauce

Staples

sugar
limes
peanut oil

Curried **Salmon Salad** with Avocado Relish

Avocados are perfect. You just cut and serve them—and they can hang out unrefrigerated for days. I eat one almost every day. I just squeeze on some fresh lime and sprinkle them with sesame seeds and a little salt. This recipe is only slightly more ambitious. –R

Serves 4

¼ cup Bertolli® extra-virgin olive oil
1   tablespoon curry powder
1   large red onion, cut into small dice
2   Granny Smith apples, peeled and cut into small dice
1¼ pounds salmon fillets, cut into large chunks
3   ripe Haas avocados
    Juice of 2 limes
2   bunches fresh cilantro, chopped
⅓   cup mayonnaise

See photo, page 179.

1. In a very large sauté pan heat the olive oil with curry powder over medium heat. When the curry powder begins to sizzle, add 1 cup of the onions and all of the apples. Season to taste with salt and pepper. Cover and cook vegetables for 2 minutes.

2. Add the salmon and season again with salt and pepper. Cover and turn heat down to low. Cook until the salmon is cooked through and the vegetables are softened, about 10 minutes. Strain the cooked mixture over a large bowl. Reserve cooking liquid and let the salmon cool slightly.

3. Halve and pit the avocados (see page 11). Scoop the flesh into a large bowl. Mix in the remaining red onions, lime juice, and cilantro. Season to taste with salt and pepper and set aside.

4. In a large bowl combine the mayonnaise with the reserved cooking liquid—it should be bright yellow. Using a spatula, gently combine the cooked salmon mixture with just enough curry mayonnaise to bind it.

5. Serve the warm salmon salad alongside the avocado relish.

Tools

very large sauté pan

Grocery List

Fresh

2 Granny Smith apples
1¼ pounds salmon fillets
3 ripe Haas avocados
2 bunches cilantro

Packaged

Staples

extra-virgin olive oil
mayonnaise/curry powder
red onion/limes

less than 15 minutes

Broiled Salmon with Turnip & Onion Relish

Friends arrived for dinner on a day which I'd taken a longer-than-I-should-have nap. I found a daikon radish and an onion in the fridge. Yikes! I grated both, cooked them with soy sauce, and grilled some steak. My friends were pretty happy—and so was I. –R

Tools

broiler pan

large sauté pan

Grocery List

Fresh

4 8-ounce boneless, skinless salmon fillets
3 white turnips
1 bunch scallions

Packaged

10-ounce bottle Kikkoman® ponzu sauce

Staples

toasted sesame oil
Vidalia onions

1. Preheat broiler on high. Season salmon with salt and pepper. Place under the broiler for about 5 minutes, or until just cooked through.

2. Meanwhile, heat a sauté pan over high heat. Add the 1 tablespoon sesame oil and the onions. Stir fry the onions until they begin to wilt, about 1 minute. Add the turnips to the pan and continue to stir-fry over high heat until the whole mixture is slightly tender but still has some bite left to it. Add the ponzu sauce to your liking and simmer for an additional 4 minutes. Turn off the heat and season generously with black pepper.

3. Serve the salmon topped with a bed of the turnip/onion mixture. Drizzle some sesame oil and ponzu sauce over everything. Scatter sliced scallions over the top and serve.

Serves 4

4 8-ounce boneless, skinless salmon fillets
   Salt and freshly ground pepper
1 tablespoon toasted sesame oil, plus more for drizzling
2 large Vidalia onions, peeled and grated (about 2 cups)
3 white turnips, peeled and grated (about 2 cups)
¼- to ½-cup Kikkoman ponzu sauce
1 bunch scallions, cut on a diagonal

"There's no such thing as the "right" way in cooking. The way that makes you happy and the people you're feeding happy is always the right way."

less than 30 minutes

Broiled Tuna with Warm Olive & Carrot Vinaigrette

Because olives are so bitter in their natural state, they're cured in a salt brine to make them palatable. In this dish, the salty olives and sweet carrots are a delicious counterpoint to the lean grilled tuna. –R

Serves 4

- 3 tablespoons butter
- 2 10-ounce bags Dole® shredded carrots or 6 large carrots, peeled and grated
- Salt and freshly ground pepper
- 2 tablespoons honey
- 1 tablespoon chopped fresh rosemary
- 4 8-ounce tuna fillets
- 6 tablespoons Bertolli® extra-virgin olive oil
- ¾ cup pitted Mediterranean olive medley
- Juice and zest of 2 lemons

1. Preheat a grill/grill pan/broiler on high.

2. Heat a large sauté pan over medium heat; add the butter and the carrots. Season to taste with salt and pepper. Pour the honey into the pan and stir until it dissolves. Cook the carrots, stirring occasionally, for 2 to 3 minutes. Add the rosemary to the pan. Toss to combine and continue to cook until the carrots are tender, about 3 minutes.

3. Meanwhile, season the tuna generously with salt and pepper. Lay the tuna on a broiler pan. Rub the fish with 2 tablespoons of the olive oil. Cook, turning once, until the tuna begins to brown and the flesh is almost cooked through, about 10 minutes.

4. In a small microwaveable bowl combine the remaining oil, olives, lemon juice and zest, and microwave on high until very warm, about 1 minute.

5. To serve, spoon a pile of carrots in the center of each plate and lay a tuna fillet on top. Liberally spoon the olive vinaigrette over the fish and serve.

See photo, page 191.

Tools

grill pan

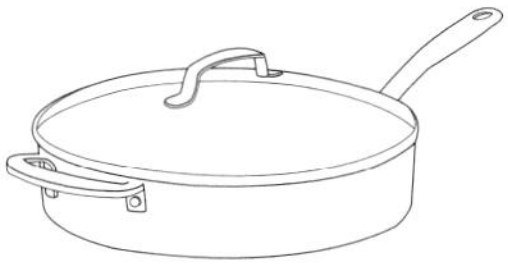

large sauté pan

Grocery List

Fresh

4 8-ounce tuna fillets

Packaged

2 10-ounce bags Dole® shredded carrots
1-ounce package fresh rosemary
12-ounce jar Mediterranean olive medley

Staples

butter/honey
extra-virgin olive oil
lemons

Grilled **Tuna Steaks** with Sweet & Sour Mangoes

less than **15** minutes

The concentrated flavor of a jam, jelly, or fruit puree is powerful. Here fresh fruit is backed up with fruit preserves. Nectars, juices, Polaner® Pourable Fruit, dried fruit—even fruit leather—can make an ordinary dish extraordinary. –R

Serves 4

4   8-ounce tuna steaks
2   tablespoons Bertolli® extra-virgin olive oil
    Salt and freshly ground pepper
4   ripe mangoes, cut into a large dice
1   medium red onion, cut into a medium dice
1   cup Aunt Jenny's® apricot & peach all natural sauce, or other sweet-and-sour fruit sauce of your choice
¼   cup white wine vinegar
1   bunch fresh basil, torn

1. Preheat a grill/grill pan/broiler on high.

2. Coat the tuna steaks with the olive oil and season generously with salt and pepper. Grill the tuna to desired doneness, about 1½ minutes per side for medium rare.

3. Meanwhile, in a large bowl toss together the mangoes, red onion, fruit sauce, vinegar, and basil. Season to taste with salt and pepper.

4. Serve tuna on top of a bed of the sweet and sour mangoes.

Tools

grill pan

Grocery List

Fresh

4 8-ounce tuna steaks
4 ripe mangoes

Packaged

17.5-ounce jar Aunt Jenny's® apricot & peach all natural sauce
1-ounce package fresh basil

Staples

extra-virgin olive oil
red onion
white wine vinegar

less than 30
minutes

Crab-Stuffed Tuna with Spinach

Tuna is delicious all on its own, but it certainly can't suffer from the addition of some sweet and delicate crabmeat. Mixing it up makes the flavor of the dish more complex—and more interesting. —R

Tools

large sauté pan

Grocery List

Fresh

8-ounces fresh crabmeat
8 4-ounce thin slices of tuna

Packaged

3-ounce package shallots
16-ounce package baby spinach
12-ounce jar Patak's® hot mango chutney

Staples

lemons
extra-virgin olive oil

1. Preheat the oven to 350°F.

2. In a medium bowl mix the crab, shallot, lemon zest and juice, and 1 tablespoon of the olive oil. Season with salt and pepper.

3. Lay four 12×14-inch squares of foil on a work surface. Lightly oil the foil with 2 tablespoons of the olive oil. Season the foil with salt and pepper. Place one piece of tuna on each piece of foil. Divide the crab mixture among the four fillets. Top each pile of crab with another tuna fillet so that the crab mixture is completely covered by the fish. Season the tuna with salt and pepper.

4. Wrap each "stuffed" tuna package tightly in the foil. Bake for about 12 minutes.

5. Meanwhile, heat a large sauté pan over high heat. Add the remaining tablespoon of olive oil and the spinach. Season lightly with salt and pepper and cook, stirring occasionally, for about 1 minute. Stir the chutney into the spinach and continue to cook until the spinach is wilted and tender, about 1 to 2 minutes.

6. When the fish is done remove the packages from oven. Very gently slide the fish out of the package onto a plate. Top with a portion of spinach. Pour the juices from the foil over the fish and serve.

Serves 4

8	ounces fresh crabmeat
1	shallot, chopped fine
	Zest of 3 lemons, juice of 1 lemon
4	tablespoons Bertolli® extra-virgin olive oil
	Salt and freshly ground pepper
	Aluminum foil
8	4-ounce thin slices of fresh tuna
16	ounces baby spinach
⅓	cup Patak's® hot mango chutney

Grilled **Tuna Steak**
with Warm Bacon & Green Pea Salad

less than 15 minutes

I worked in a 4-star restaurant that used frozen peas in its cooking. Frozen peas at a 4-star restaurant? When I tasted them I understood. Because the sugar converts to starch so quickly, frozen peas taste better than fresh more often than not. –R

Serves 4

- ⅓   **pound bacon, cut into small chunks**
- 1   **10-ounce package frozen peas**
      Salt and freshly ground pepper
- 2   **tablespoons chopped fresh tarragon**
- 4   **8-ounce tuna steaks**
- 2   **tablespoons Bertolli® extra-virgin olive oil**

1. Preheat a grill/grill pan/broiler on high.

2. Heat a large sauté pan over medium heat. Add the bacon to the pan and cook, stirring occasionally, until it begins to brown, about 4 minutes. Add the peas to the pan and season with salt and pepper. Stir the peas to evenly coat them with the rendered bacon fat. Add the tarragon, cover with a lid, and cook until the peas are tender and hot throughout, about 5 minutes.

3. Coat the tuna steaks with the olive oil and season generously with salt and pepper. Grill the fish to desired doneness, about 1½ minutes per side for medium rare.

4. Top the tuna with the warm bacon and green pea salad and serve.

Tools

grill pan

large sauté pan

Grocery List

Fresh

⅓ pound bacon
4 8-ounce tuna steaks

Packaged

10-ounce package frozen peas
1-ounce package fresh tarragon

Staples

extra-virgin olive oil

Grilled **Tuna Steaks** with Fresh Salsa Verde

The word tomatillo may mean "little tomato, but I wouldn't think of it as a tomato at all. The flavor of a tomatillo can run the gamut from sweet as a cherry to sour and lemony as a pickle—which you might have noticed if you eat a lot of salsa verde. –R

Tools

food processor

large sauté pan

Grocery List

Fresh

1½ pounds tomatillos
2 small jalapeño peppers
1 bunch cilantro
4 8-ounce tuna steaks

Packaged

Staples

lime/onion
sugar
extra-virgin olive oil

1. Preheat the broiler on high.

2. Lay the tomatillos, cut side down, on a baking sheet. Place the sheet under the broiler, and cook until the tomatillo skins start to blacken, blister, and char, about 10 minutes.

3. Place the tomatillos, onion, jalapeños, cilantro, sugar, and 2 tablespoons of the olive oil in a food processor or blender. Pulse until all ingredients are roughly chopped and mixed. Season to taste with salt and set aside.

4. Heat a large sauté pan over high heat. Add the remaining 2 tablespoons of oil. Season the tuna generously with salt and pepper. When the oil gets slightly smoky, carefully lay the tuna steaks in the pan. Cook for about 1½ to 2 minutes per side for rare to medium rare.

5. Serve tuna topped with the salsa verde.

Serves 4

1½ pounds tomatillos, husks removed, cut in half
Juice of 1 lime
1 medium to large onion, roughly chopped
2 small jalapeño peppers, stemmed, seeded, and chopped
⅔ cup chopped fresh cilantro
½ teaspoon sugar
4 tablespoons Bertolli® extra-virgin olive oil
Salt and freshly ground pepper
4 8-ounce tuna steaks, about 1 inch thick

Seared & Sliced Tuna
with Radishes & Snow Peas

less than 15 minutes

Radishes are just as delicious cooked as they are raw. You can sauté radishes with some butter and you'll have a great tasting, easy side dish. The only trick is not to overcook them because you want to preserve that sharp spiciness the radish is known for. —R

Serves 4

¼ cup Bertolli® extra-virgin olive oil

1½ pounds sushi-grade tuna, cut into 2 blocks

Salt and freshly ground pepper

2 15-ounce cans sweet potatoes, drained

1 bunch radishes

½ cup Kikkoman® ponzu sauce

2 cups snow peas, cut into small chunks

2 small bunches scallions, cut on a diagonal

See photo, page 187.

1. Heat a large sauté pan over high heat and let it get very hot. Pour 2 tablespoons of the olive oil into the hot pan.

2. Season the tuna with salt and pepper. Carefully place the tuna blocks in the pan and sear each side. It should take about 30 seconds per side if the pan is hot.

3. Remove the tuna from the pan. Add the sweet potatoes to the pan and heat, stirring, until hot throughout. Divide the sweet potatoes evenly among four plates.

4. Meanwhile, slice the tuna as thinly as possible and arrange on top of the sweet potatoes so that the slices don't overlap. Place the radishes in a sealable plastic bag and crush with the bottom of a small skillet. You want to have about 1 cup of crushed radishes.

5. Heat the remaining olive oil and ponzu sauce in a small saucepan until just simmering. Add the crushed radishes and turn heat up to high. When the mixture just boils turn off the heat and add the snow peas. Spoon the hot mixture evenly over the tuna to finish "cooking" it.

6. Scatter the scallions generously over the tuna and serve immediately.

Tools

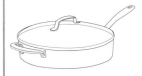

large sauté pan

small saucepan

Grocery List

Fresh

1½ pounds sushi-grade tuna
1 bunch radishes
2 cups snow peas
2 small bunches scallions

Packaged

2 15-ounce cans sweet potatoes
12-ounce jar Kikkoman® ponzu sauce

Staples

extra-virgin olive oil

Sweet & Sour Tuna

Although I don't always call it out in the title of the recipe, there is a sweet and sour element in nearly everything I make. Every dish is some combination of four basic flavors—sour, salt, sweet, and bitter. The better the balance among flavors in a dish, the better it is. —R

Tools

grill pan

Grocery List

Fresh

1 bunch flat-leaf parsley
1 pound radishes
4 large prepared tuna kabobs
(2 pounds total)

Packaged

15-ounce package Sun-Maid®
golden raisins
1-ounce package fresh
rosemary

Staples

red wine vinegar
extra-virgin olive oil

1. Preheat a grill/grill pan/broiler on high.

2. In a medium microwaveable bowl combine raisins and vinegar. Microwave on high for 2 minutes or until mixture is warm and raisins are plump. Add 3 tablespoons of the olive oil, the rosemary, and the parsley.

3. Meanwhile, place the radishes in a sealable plastic bag and crush with the bottom of a small skillet. Add the crushed radishes to the raisins and toss to combine. Season to taste with salt and pepper and set aside at room temperature.

4. Brush the tuna kabobs with the remaining tablespoon of olive oil and season with salt and pepper. Grill the tuna just until cooked through, about 1½ to 2 minutes per side. Serve tuna with the radish salad.

Serves 4

1 cup Sun-Maid® golden raisins
¼ cup red wine vinegar
4 tablespoons Bertolli® extra-virgin olive oil
2 tablespoons chopped fresh rosemary
2 tablespoons chopped fresh flat-leaf parsley
1 pound radishes, trimmed and quartered
Salt and freshly ground pepper
4 large prepared tuna kabobs (2 pounds total)

Tuna & Tomatoes with Creamy Polenta

less than 15 minutes

Polenta is one of my favorite side dishes. Even without the addition of any fat, it has a rich, creamy texture. And there's no reason to spend 30 to 40 minutes cooking it from scratch because there are great instant polenta products just about everywhere. –R

Serves 4

- 2 cups instant polenta
- 3 tablespoons Bertolli® extra-virgin olive oil
- 4 8-ounce albacore tuna steaks, about 1 inch thick Salt and freshly ground pepper
- 1½ cups Victoria® tomato-basil sauce
- ½ cup grated Parmigiano-Reggiano cheese
- ½ cup chopped fresh basil

1. In a large saucepan cook the polenta according to the package directions.

2. Meanwhile, heat a large sauté pan over high heat. Add the olive oil to the pan and allow it to get very hot.

3. Dab the tuna dry with a clean paper towel. Season the tuna with salt and pepper. Carefully place the tuna in the pan and sear one side for about 45 seconds to 1 minute. Turn the tuna over and sear for another 30 seconds. Add the tomato-basil sauce to the pan and bring to a gentle simmer.

4. Continue cooking until all of the sauce is heated through, about 2 to 3 minutes. Tuna should be cooked to medium rare or medium by this point.

5. Meanwhile, stir the cheese into the polenta. Divide the polenta among four pasta bowls.

6. Place the tuna steaks on top of the polenta and spoon some tomato sauce on top. Sprinkle tuna and polenta with basil and serve.

Tools

large saucepan

large sauté pan

Grocery List

Fresh

4 8-ounce Albacore tuna steaks

Packaged

20-ounce box instant polenta
24.7-ounce jar Victoria®
tomato-basil sauce
1-ounce package fresh basil

Staples

extra-virgin olive oil
Parmigiano-Reggiano cheese

less than 15
minutes

Tuna Steaks with Red Cabbage Slaw

Cabbage is great raw, cooked, and everything in between. Unlike avocado or artichokes, it has a lean, almost squeaky quality to it—so I like to dress it with something rich, like mayonnaise or bacon. Here I use sour cream. —R

Tools

grill pan

large sauté pan

Grocery List

Fresh

4 8-ounce tuna steaks
1 bunch chives

Packaged

15-ounce package Sun-Maid®
golden raisins
2 10-ounce packages Dole®
shredded red cabbage

Staples

cider vinegar
Classico olive oil
sour cream

1. Preheat grill/grill pan/broiler on high.

2. Combine raisins and vinegar in a medium bowl and microwave on high until raisins begin to plump, about 1½ minutes.

3. Heat 2 tablespoons of the oil in a large sauté pan. Add the cabbage and sauté, stirring occasionally, for about 2 minutes, or until cabbage just starts to get tender but is still very crunchy. Add the raisins and vinegar. Season to taste with salt and pepper. Stir in sour cream.

4. Season tuna generously with salt and pepper and coat with remaining olive oil. Grill about 4 minutes per side or until just cooked through.

5. Divide slaw among four plates. Add a tuna steak to each plate. Sprinkle everything with chives and serve.

Serves 4

¾ cup Sun-Maid® golden
    raisins
½ cup cider vinegar
¼ cup Bertolli® Classico olive
    oil
2 10-ounce packages Dole®
    shredded red cabbage
    Salt and freshly ground
    pepper
¾ cup sour cream
4 8-ounce tuna steaks
1 bunch chives, chopped

Tuna with Lemon, Capers & Parsley

less than 15 minutes

A caper is the bud of the caper bush, which is native to the Mediterranean. It's almost always pickled in a salty brine. The smallest capers are classified as "nonpareils" and are considered the best. I like them because they distribute themselves evenly. —R

Serves 4

1½ pounds tuna, cut into
        8 pieces, about ¾ inch
        thick
        Salt and freshly ground
        pepper
1   cup all-purpose flour
2   eggs, beaten well
12   tablespoons butter
        (1½ sticks)
2   tablespoons Amore®
        garlic paste or 6 garlic
        cloves, chopped
½   cup lemon juice
¼   cup chopped capers
¼   cup chopped fresh
        flat-leaf parsley

1. Heat a large sauté pan over medium heat.

2. Season the tuna on both sides with salt and pepper. Dredge the tuna in the flour and shake off excess. In a large, shallow dish dip tuna into the beaten eggs.

3. Add half the butter to the pan. Before it melts completely, add half of the tuna to the pan and cook until eggs firm up and brown slightly, about 2½ minutes per side. Remove tuna from pan and repeat process with remaining tuna. Arrange cooked tuna on a platter.

4. Add the remaining butter to the pan, then the garlic. Cook, stirring, until butter is light golden brown. Add lemon juice. Turn the heat up and simmer until lemon juice is slightly reduced and sauce has thickened somewhat, about 1½ minutes. Add capers to sauce and season to taste with salt and pepper.

5. Stir parsley into sauce and pour over the fish.

Tools

large sauté pan

Grocery List

Fresh

1½ pounds tuna
1 bunch flat-leaf parsley

Packaged

3.15-ounce tube Amore® garlic paste

Staples

flour/eggs
butter/lemons
capers

less than 30 minutes

Tuna & Tomatoes Poached in Olive Oil

Poaching in fat seems excessive—but it's not. Oil, like a salt crust or a vacuum-sealed pouch, completely seals in the fish. There's no oxygen to dry it out or water to bleed out flavor. I have cooked fish in goose fat, lard, and olive oil—and the results are awesome. —R

Tools

Dutch oven

medium sauté pan

Grocery List

Fresh

4 6-ounce tuna fillets
2 large beefsteak or heirloom tomatoes
¼ pound thick-sliced bacon

Packaged

2 32-ounce bottles Bertolli® extra light tasting olive oil
3.15-ounce tube Amore® garlic paste
6-ounce package baby spinach

Staples

1. In a Dutch oven warm the olive oil over medium heat to 140°F. Season the tuna with salt and pepper and add to the pot. Add the tomatoes, making sure everthing is submerged. Cook until fish is done, about 8 to 10 minutes for medium. Watch the oil temperature carefully throughout the cooking time so you don't overcook the tuna. Remove fish and tomatoes from the oil.

2. Meanwhile, heat a medium sauté pan over medium-high heat. Add the bacon and cook, stirring, until brown and crispy, about 3 minutes. Remove the bacon from the pan and drain on a paper towel-lined plate. Pour out most of the bacon fat. Put the pan back on the heat. Add garlic and cook, stirring, until slightly brown, about 1 minute. Add the spinach and cook, stirring occasionally, until wilted, about 2 minutes. Season to taste with salt and pepper.

3. Divide spinach among four plates. Place tuna on the spinach. Top with a tomato slice. Sprinkle with bacon and serve.

Serves 4

2	quarts Bertolli® extra light tasting olive oil (not extra virgin)
4	6-ounce tuna fillets
	Salt and freshly ground pepper
2	large beefsteak or heirloom tomatoes, cored and cut into 1-inch slices
¼	pound thick-sliced bacon, cut into chunks
2	teaspoons Amore® garlic paste or 2 garlic cloves, sliced thin
1	6-ounce bag baby spinach

Tuna with Clams, Mushrooms, & Andouille Sausage

less than 15 minutes

Clams truly taste of the sea. They're sweet, briny, and intense. With all the farmed fish out there, it's nice to be able to count on an ingredient that always delivers. —R

Serves 4

¼ cup Bertolli® extra-virgin olive oil

1 pound mixed mushrooms, cleaned and trimmed

¼ pound andouille sausage, finely chopped

2 teaspoons Amore® garlic paste or 2 garlic cloves, smashed

Salt and freshly ground pepper

1 medium tomato, chopped

½ cup dry white wine

2 pounds fresh Manila or littleneck clams in the shell, scrubbed clean

2 pounds fresh tuna, cut into 8 portions

See photo, page 186.

1. In a large, heavy-bottomed sauté pan heat olive oil over high heat. Add mushrooms, sausage, and garlic. Season with salt and pepper. Reduce the heat to medium, cover tightly, and cook on low heat until tender but not browned, about 2 minutes.

2. Add the tomato, wine, and clams. Bring to a boil, then reduce the heat and simmer, covered, until clams just open, about 3 to 4 minutes.

3. Season the tuna with a generous pinch of salt and a sprinkle of pepper. Place the tuna in the pan and cook to desired doneness, about 3 minutes for rare.

4. Divide tuna among four large, shallow soup bowls or pasta plates. Spoon clams and broth on top and serve.

Tools

large sauté pan

Grocery List

Fresh

1 pound mixed mushrooms
¼ pound andouille sausage
1 medium tomato
2 pounds Manila or little neck clams in the shell
2 pounds tuna

Packaged

3.15-ounce tube Amore® garlic paste

Staples

extra-virgin olive oil
garlic
dry white wine

less than 30 minutes

Tuna and Potatoes alla Mama

My mother had a knack for recreating dishes from her childhood in Italy using ingredients available to her in this country. She always had a full-time job when I was a kid so she had to be quick and practical—which is why I call for onion and garlic powder here. —R

Tools

9×13-inch baking dish

broiler pan

Grocery List

Fresh

5 large Idaho potatoes
4 8-ounce tuna steaks

Packaged

8-ounce can Progresso®
Italian-style bread crumbs
16-ounce package shredded
mozzarella
1-ounce package fresh
oregano

Staples

extra-virgin olive oil/lemons
onion powder/garlic powder
crushed red pepper flakes

1. Preheat the broiler to 550°F.

2. In a large bowl toss together the potatoes, ¼ cup of the olive oil, and the breadcrumbs. The potatoes should have a light coating of the mixture. Spread potatoes in a microwaveable 9×3-inch baking dish and season generously with salt and pepper.

3. Microwave potatoes on high for about 10 minutes or until tender, turning the pan 180° halfway through cooking time. Remove from the microwave and sprinkle with the mozzarella. Set aside.

4. In a small bowl mix together the remaining olive oil, oregano, onion and garlic powders, red pepper flakes, and salt and pepper to taste. Coat both sides of the tuna generously with this mixture. Place the steaks under the broiler. Cook for about 2½ minutes per side for medium rare.

5. During the last minute or so, place the potato dish under the broiler alongside the fish. Broil until the cheese melts and begins to brown.

6. Serve tuna with potatoes and lemon wedges.

Serves 4

5   large Idaho potatoes, cut
    into wedges
⅓   cup Bertolli® extra-virgin
    olive oil
½   cup Progresso® Italian-
    Style breadcrumbs
    Salt and freshly ground
    pepper
2   cups shredded mozzarella
    (whole milk, low
    moisture if possible)
3   tablespoons chopped
    fresh oregano
1   tablespoon onion powder
1   tablespoon garlic powder
1   teaspoon crushed red
    pepper flakes
4   8-ounce tuna steaks,
    about 1 inch thick
2   lemons, cut into wedges

R

SHELLFISH

“There's no mistake in cooking that can't be fixed.”

less than 30
minutes

Crispy **Fried Shrimp** with Warm Coleslaw

Coleslaw mix is very practical and can be turned into an easy vegetable side. This version is unexpected in all kinds of good ways—warm instead of cold, and dressed with a bacon-red wine vinaigrette instead of the standard mayo-based dressing. —R

Tools

Dutch oven

large sauté pan

Grocery List

Fresh

1 pound thick-cut bacon
16 jumbo shrimp
1 bunch chives

Packaged

64-ounce container corn oil
2 packages coleslaw mix
2-pound container fine cornmeal

Staples

butter
red wine vinegar
eggs

1. In a heavy-bottomed Dutch oven heat the oil to 375°F.

2. While oil is heating, heat a large sauté pan over medium heat. Add the butter, then the bacon, and stir often until bacon begins to render its fat. Add the cabbage to the pan and season generously with salt and pepper. Cook the cabbage mixture, stirring occasionally, until tender, about 6 to 8 minutes. Add a little water if the pan starts to go dry. When cabbage is tender, stir in the vinegar.

3. Meanwhile, in a shallow dish season the cornmeal with salt and pepper. Dip the shrimp in the beaten eggs, turning to coat, then dredge in cornmeal. Set each shrimp aside as you finish it. When all of the shrimp are coated, very carefully lay the shrimp in the oil a few at a time and fry until crispy and golden brown, about 2 minutes. Drain on a paper towel-lined plate. Season to taste with salt and pepper, if necessary.

4. Stir chives into the warm cabbage and season to taste with salt and pepper. Serve hot shrimp on a bed of the cabbage with a drizzle of the bacon pan juices.

Serves 4

½ gallon corn oil, for frying
8 tablespoons butter (1 stick)
1 pound thick-cut bacon, cut into small chunks
1½ pounds coleslaw mix
 Salt and freshly ground pepper
¼ cup red wine vinegar
1 cup fine cornmeal
16 jumbo shrimp, peeled and deveined, tails removed
2 eggs, well beaten
4 tablespoons finely chopped fresh chives

See photos, pages 182-83.

Shrimp and Cherry Tomatoes

less than 15 minutes

I once served a dish of cherry tomatoes and balsamic vinegar out of desperation. I had nothing else available. Both my guests and I loved it. Tomatoes and balsamic vinegar get along well together, so even though it was just two ingredients it tasted like a lot more. —R

Serves 4

Aluminum foil

1½ pounds broccoli rabe, washed, trimmed of rough stems and leaves, and cut into small pieces

1 red onion, peeled, halved, and sliced thin

16 cherry tomatoes, stemmed

½ cup fresh basil, torn
Salt and freshly ground pepper

4 tablespoons Bertolli® extra-virgin olive oil

4 teaspoons balsamic vinegar, plus more for drizzling

2 pounds large shrimp, peeled and deveined, tails removed

1. Preheat oven to 400°F.

2. On a work surface lay out eight 12-inch pieces of foil.

3. In a medium bowl, combine the broccoli rabe, onion, tomatoes, and half of the basil. Season to taste with salt and pepper. Drizzle with 1 tablespoon of olive oil and a splash of vinegar.

4. Pile a mound of vegetables on half of the sheets of foil. Season the shrimp on both sides with salt and pepper and place on top of the vegetables. Drizzle each pile with 1 teaspoon of the remaining olive oil and 1 teaspoon of the remaining vinegar. Use the remaining pieces of foil to seal the pouches completely.

5. Place the pouches on a baking sheet. Bake for 10 minutes.

6. To serve, put the pouches on each of four plates and open them at the table. Garnish with remaining basil and a final drizzle of the remaining olive oil.

Tools

baking sheet

Grocery List

Fresh

1½ pounds broccoli rabe
½ pound cherry tomatoes
2 pounds large shrimp

Packaged

1-ounce package fresh basil

Staples

red onion
extra-virgin olive oil
balsamic vinegar

Jumbo Shrimp and Red Swiss Chard

Swiss chard is from the same vegetable family as beets, so when you use red Swiss chard the color will run just like it does with beets. Swiss chard—like beets—has a rich, deep, almost meaty flavor that makes a great sauce for this dish. —R

Tools

large sauté pan

food processor

Grocery List

Fresh

1 bunch red Swiss chard
2 pounds jumbo shrimp
1 bunch chives
2 to 4 heads Bibb lettuce

Packaged

8-ounce carton mascarpone
1-ounce package fresh basil

Staples

red wine vinegar
extra-virgin olive oil
flour/butter/lemons

1. Pour the vinegar into a large sauté pan and bring to a simmer. Toss in the Swiss chard and season lightly with salt and pepper. Simmer gently until the Swiss chard is tender, about 15 minutes. (If the pan becomes too dry, add ¼ cup water.) Cool the Swiss chard mixture slightly.

2. Add Swiss chard and mascarpone to the bowl of a food processor. Puree just until mixture is completely blended.

3. Heat the olive oil in a large sauté pan until very hot. Season the shrimp generously with salt and pepper and dust just one side with flour. Place shrimp in the pan, flour side down. Allow them to get a deep golden brown, about 2 minutes.

4. Flip the shrimp and add the butter to the pan. The butter will turn brown and foam. Using a large spoon baste the shrimp with the butter and continue cooking for 3 minutes. Turn off heat and drain the butter from the pan. Add the Swiss chard mixture to the pan and swirl to liquefy the sauce and coat the shrimp.

5. Sprinkle with chives and basil and season to taste with salt and pepper, if necessary. Place one lettuce half on each plate and spoon the shrimp and Swiss chard sauce on top. Serve immediately, with lemon wedges for squeezing on the shrimp, if desired.

Serves 4

⅓ cup red wine vinegar

4 cups red Swiss chard, washed and cut into small chunks

Salt and freshly ground pepper

½ cup mascarpone

2 tablespoons Bertolli® extra-virgin olive oil

2 pounds jumbo shrimp, peeled and deveined, tails removed

1 cup all-purpose flour

4 tablespoons butter

2 tablespoons chopped fresh chives

2 tablespoons chopped fresh basil

2 to 4 heads of Bibb lettuce (depends on their size), washed and cut in half

Lemon wedges (optional)

Shrimp Parmigiano
with White Beans and Olives

less than 15
minutes

There's Chicken Parmigiano and Eggplant Parmigiano—why not Shrimp Parmigiano? I am keeping it somewhat pure, though, by only using Parmigiano-Reggiano and not mozzarella. If you can't find olive spread, just throw some chopped olives into the sauce. —R

Serves 4

- 2 15-ounce cans Progresso® cannellini beans, rinsed and drained
- 2 cups Victoria® marinara sauce, or marinara of your choice
- ½ cup Delallo® olive bruschetta topping, or olive condiment of your choice
   Salt and freshly ground pepper
- 2 tablespoons Bertolli® extra-virgin olive oil
- 1½ pounds medium shrimp, peeled and deveined, tails removed
- 1 cup grated Parmigiano-Reggiano cheese
- ¼ cup chopped fresh flat-leaf parsley

1. Preheat the broiler on high.

2. In a large sauté pan heat the beans, marinara, and olive topping over medium-high heat. Season to taste with salt and pepper, if necessary.

3. While the bean stew is simmering brush a foil-lined broiler pan with the oil. Arrange the shrimp on the foil and season lightly with salt and pepper. Sprinkle the shrimp evenly with the cheese.

4. Place the shrimp under the broiler for 3 to 5 minutes. The cheese should bubble and turn golden brown.

5. Divide the bean stew among four large bowls and lay the shrimp on top. Sprinkle with parsley and serve.

Tools

large sauté pan

broiler pan

Grocery List

Fresh

1½ pounds medium shrimp
1 bunch parsley

Packaged

2 15-ounce cans Progresso®
cannellini beans
24-ounce jar Victoria®
marinana sauce
10-ounce jar Delallo® olive
bruschetta topping

Staples

extra-virgin olive oil
Parmigiano-Reggiano cheese

Sweet and Sticky **Coconut Shrimp**

If you're going to make coconut shrimp, there's only one way to do it. You've got to use Coco Lopez®. It's normally used for making drinks, but so what? Frying shredded coconut makes it taste like a greasy Brillo® pad. Stay away from it and take a closer look at your bar. –R

Tools

large sauté pan

Grocery List

Fresh

2 pounds jumbo shrimp
1 bunch cilantro

Packaged

3.15-ounce tube Amore® garlic paste
12-ounce package Dole® broccoli slaw mix
15-ounce can Coco Lopez®

Staples

extra-virgin olive oil
limes

1. Heat a large sauté pan over very high heat.

2. Season the shrimp with salt and pepper. Add the oil, garlic, and shrimp to the pan. Sauté the shrimp for 30 seconds on each side. Toss in broccoli slaw and spoon on the Coco Lopez®. Cook, stirring often, for about 2½ minutes or until mixture is thick and the shrimp are just cooked through.

3. Drizzle in the fresh lime juice and season to taste with salt and pepper.

4. Sprinkle the cilantro over the shrimp and serve.

Serves 4

2   pounds jumbo shrimp, peeled and deveined, tails removed
    Salt and freshly ground pepper
2   tablespoons Bertolli® extra-virgin olive oil
4   teaspoons Amore® garlic paste or 4 garlic cloves, chopped
2   10-ounce bags Dole® broccoli slaw
¾   cup Coco Lopez®
¼   cup fresh lime juice
⅓   cup chopped fresh cilantro

Shrimp with Beets and Butter Lettuce

The first time I saw a sauce made from butter lettuce, I was dining at one of the fanciest restaurants in the world. It was served with squab, and boy was I impressed. At that moment I decided to shamelessly "liberate" that idea. Here's the result of my pilfering. —R

Serves 4

2   pounds medium shrimp, peeled and deveined, tails removed
3   tablespoons unsalted butter
    Salt and freshly ground pepper
    Juice and zest of 1 lemon
2   cups Aunt Nellie's® Harvard beets, at room temperature
4   heads butter lettuce or other delicately flavored greens (like Boston lettuce), washed and torn into bite-size pieces

1. Dry shrimp thoroughly with paper towels.

2. Heat a sauté pan over high heat. When it's hot, add 2 tablespoons of the butter. As the butter foams, sprinkle the shrimp with salt and pepper and add immediately to the pan. Do not disturb the shrimp for 30 seconds. After 30 seconds loosen the shrimp with a spatula and swirl the pan in a circular motion to roll the shrimp. This will cause all of the surface areas of the shrimp to come in contact with the hot pan, and they'll turn a light golden brown. The whole process should take no more than 3 minutes.

3. Add lemon juice, half of the zest, and the remaining 1 tablespoon butter. Stir vigorously to release any browned bits. Season to taste with salt and pepper.

4. In a large bowl toss the beets with the lettuce. Gently fold in the warm shrimp and lemon sauce.

5. Sprinkle with the remaining lemon zest and serve immediately, while shrimp are still warm.

Tools

sauté pan

Grocery List

Fresh

2 pounds medium shrimp
4 heads butter lettuce

Packaged

15.5-ounce jar Aunt Nellie's® Harvard beets

Staples

unsalted butter
lemon

Jumbo Shrimp
with Hot and Sour Honey Glaze

The sweetness of honey is great paired with vermouth. I cook with vermouth a lot. It's a fortified wine (it has some spirits added) flavored with between 15 and 55 different botanicals. Adding one spoon of vermouth is like adding all those flavors. —R

Tools

large sauté pan

Grocery List

Fresh

8 medium Cubanelle peppers
2 pounds large shrimp, peeled, deveined, tails removed

Packaged

750 ml. bottle Martini & Rossi® bianco vermouth

Staples

extra-virgin olive oil
honey/limes
crushed red pepper

1. In a large sauté pan heat 1 cup of the olive oil on high heat. When the oil begins to smoke, carefully lay the peppers in the pan. Cook, turning often, until the skins blister and the flesh is tender, about 5 minutes. Drain the peppers on a paper towel-lined plate. When the peppers are cool enough to handle, cut them in half lengthwise.

2. Meanwhile, combine honey, vermouth, lime juice, and crushed red pepper in a small bowl.

3. Drain the oil from the sauté pan and wipe clean with a paper towel. Heat the remaining oil in the pan over medium heat. Season shrimp with salt and pepper. Sauté the shrimp until they are just cooked through, about 2 to 3 minutes.

4. Lay the peppers in the pan and pour over the honey glaze to cover everything completely. Heat through. Season to taste with salt and pepper, if necessary.

5. Divide the peppers among four plates. Pile the shrimp on top of the peppers. Place a couple of lime wedges on each plate. Sprinkle shrimp and peppers with lime zest and serve.

Serves 4

1¼	cup Bertolli® extra-virgin olive oil
8	medium Cubanelle peppers, stemmed and seeded
1	cup honey
4	tablespoons Martini & Rossi® bianco vermouth
	Juice and zest of 2 limes
¾	teaspoon crushed red pepper
2	pounds large shrimp, peeled and deveined, tails removed
	Salt and freshly ground pepper
2	limes, cut into wedges

Shrimp Scampi over Grilled Tomatoes

Scampi are a variety of shellfish found in the southern Italian Mediterranean. And while true scampi are a real treasure (I urge you to go see for yourself someday) because they're fattier—and therefore richer—garlic and olive oil make anything taste good. –R

Serves 4

½ cup **Bertolli® extra-virgin olive oil**

2 tablespoons **Amore® garlic paste or 6 cloves garlic, finely chopped**

4 **large beefsteak tomatoes, halved horizontally**
   Salt and freshly ground pepper

4 **tablespoons butter (½ stick)**

1½ **pounds very large shrimp, peeled and deveined, tails removed**
   Juice of 3 lemons

⅓ **cup chopped fresh flat-leaf parsley**

1. Heat a grill pan/broiler/grill on high.

2. In a small bowl, combine 2 tablespoons of the olive oil with ½ tablespoon of the garlic.

3. Brush the tomatoes with the garlic oil and season to taste with salt and pepper. Grill until slightly charred all over, about 2 to 3 minutes per side. Set aside.

4. Meanwhile, in a large sauté pan heat the butter and the remaining olive oil over medium heat. Add the remaining garlic and cook, stirring constantly, for about 30 seconds. Do not allow garlic to brown.

5. Season the shrimp with salt and pepper and add to pan. After about 1½ minutes, flip shrimp and add the lemon juice to the pan. Simmer until shrimp are just cooked through, about 1½ more minutes. Add parsley to pan and season to taste with salt and pepper.

6. Place two tomato halves on each of four plates. Divide the shrimp evenly over the tomatoes. Generously spoon the sauce over the top of everything and serve.

Tools

grill pan

large sauté pan

Grocery List

Fresh

4 large beefsteak tomatoes
1½ pounds very large shrimp,
1 bunch parsley

Packaged

3.15-ounce tube Amore®garlic paste

Staples

extra-virgin olive oil
butter
lemons

Shrimp and Red Onion Pie

You could call this a quiche if you wanted to, but I like the idea of pie for dinner. It's made with a prepared pie crust that comes in an aluminum pan, so you don't even have a pan to wash. Serve it with a salad and some nice white wine, and it's happiness all around. –R

Tools

large sauté pan

Grocery List

Fresh

8 slices bacon
1 pound small shrimp

Packaged

1 unbaked 9-inch piecrust
1 pint half-and-half

Staples

eggs
red onion

1. Preheat oven to 450°F.

2. Prick the surface of the piecrust with a fork and bake for 5 minutes. Remove from oven and turn the temperature down to 375°F.

3. Mix the eggs with the half-and-half. Season with the salt and pepper to taste. Set aside.

4. In a large sauté pan cook the bacon over medium heat until almost crisp, about 3 minutes. Drain the bacon on a paper towel-lined plate and set aside. Add the onion to bacon fat, season with salt and pepper, and cook over medium heat until tender and slightly caramelized, about 6 to 8 minutes. Turn the heat up to high and add the shrimp to the pan. Cover and steam shrimp about 2 minutes. Toss the bacon back in with the onion and shrimp.

5. Arrange the shrimp mixture evenly in the bottom of the pastry shell. Pour the egg mixture into the shell and bake for about 30 to 35 minutes, or until the center is set.

6. Allow pie to cool slightly before cutting and serving.

Serves 4

1 unbaked 9-inch piecrust
  Salt and freshly ground pepper
4 eggs, well beaten
1 cup half-and-half
¼ teaspoon salt
  Freshly ground pepper
8 slices bacon, sliced into ½-inch pieces
1 red onion, thinly sliced
1 pound fresh small shrimp, peeled and deveined, tails removed

See photo, page 190.

Shrimp Pappardelle with Smoky Peppers

I use bacon a lot. The fat tastes great, the texture is unique, and that smoky-salt flavor is hard to find in any other ingredient. I get puzzled looks when I use it in fish dishes, but this dish wouldn't be the same without the smokiness the bacon adds to the sauce. —R

Serves 4

- 26 ounces fresh pappardelle pasta or 16 ounces dried egg pasta
- 1 pound small shrimp, peeled and deveined, tails removed
- 6 ounces sliced smoked bacon, cut into small chunks
- 2 tablespoons Amore® garlic paste or 6 garlic cloves, chopped
- 1 tablespoon Amore® anchovy paste
- 1¼ cups Mancini® pickled red peppers or pimientos, drained
- 2 cups Victoria® Fra Diavolo sauce
  Salt and freshly ground pepper

1. Bring a large pot of salted water to a boil. Cook pasta according to package instructions, adding shrimp to the pasta the last 3 minutes of cooking. Drain, reserving a cup or so of the cooking water.

2. Meanwhile, in a large saucepan cook bacon over high heat until it's translucent but not crispy, about 1 to 2 minutes. Add the garlic paste and sauté, stirring, for 30 seconds. Add the anchovy paste and do the same. Add the peppers and Fra Diavolo sauce and simmer for 5 minutes.

3. Add the cooked pasta and shrimp to the pan and toss well to combine. (You may add a little bit of the pasta cooking water to loosen the sauce up, if necessary.) Season with salt and lots of pepper and serve.

Tools

stockpot

large saucepan

Grocery List

Fresh

26 ounces fresh pappardelle pasta
1 pound small shrimp
6 ounces sliced smoked bacon

Packaged

3.15-ounce tube Amore® garlic paste
3.15-ounce tube Amore® anchovy paste
12-ounce jar Mancini® pickled red peppers
24-ounce jar Victoria® Fra Diavolo sauce

Staples

Spaghetti and **Shrimp** with Spring Vegetables

My mom makes a dish of spaghetti and spaghetti squash by adding the squash to the pasta water right before the pasta is done. As a chef who's always looking to shave minutes off cooking times, I thought this was great. Guess you never stop learning from your mom. –R

Tools

stockpot

large sauté pan

Grocery List

Fresh

1 pound medium shrimp
1 pound pencil-thin asparagus
1 tomato
1 bunch flat-leaf parsley

Packaged

1 pound dried spaghetti
3.15-ounce tube Amore® garlic paste

Staples

extra-virgin olive oil/onions
white wine/crushed red pepper flakes
Parmigiano-Reggiano cheese

1. Cook the pasta according to the package directions, in heavily salted water. When the pasta is almost cooked, add the shrimp and cook for an additional 3 minutes. Add the asparagus and cook another 1 to 2 minutes. Drain everything, reserving 1 cup of the cooking liquid.

2. Meanwhile, heat a large sauté pan over high heat. When the pan is hot, add 2 tablespoons of the olive oil. Add the onions and sauté until translucent, about 2 minutes. Add the garlic and sauté until fragrant, about 1 minute. Season to taste with salt and pepper. Add the tomato and wine and simmer until the wine is almost evaporated, about 2 minutes.

3. Add the pasta mixture with a little bit of the cooking liquid to the sauté pan. Add the cheese, parsley, and crushed red pepper. Toss gently until everything is well combined and sauce is slightly thickened. Season to taste with salt and pepper, if necessary, and serve.

Serves 4

- 1 pound dried spaghetti
  Salt
- 1 pound medium shrimp, peeled and deveined, tails removed
- 1 pound pencil-thin asparagus, tips only (about 4 inches)
- 4 tablespoons Bertolli® extra-virgin olive oil
- 1½ onions, chopped
- 1 teaspoon Amore® garlic paste or 1 clove garlic, chopped
  Freshly ground black pepper
- ¼ cup chopped tomato
- ⅓ cup dry white wine
- ½ cup Parmigiano-Reggiano cheese
- 1 cup chopped fresh flat-leaf parsley
- ⅛ teaspoon crushed red pepper flakes

See photo, page 180

Shrimp and Fennel Stew

A lot of people don't know what to do with fennel. Italians eat it raw at the end of meals as a source of fiber for digestion and as a breath freshener. It's also wonderful in cooked dishes. —R

Serves 4

- ⅓ cup Bertolli® extra-virgin olive oil
- 24 very large shrimp, peeled and deveined, tails removed
-   Salt and freshly ground pepper
- 1 onion, sliced very thin
- 1 large head fennel, sliced very thin crosswise
- 2 tablespoons Amore® garlic paste or 6 garlic cloves, chopped
- 2 ounces Pernod®
- ½ cup frozen orange juice concentrate
- 1 cup diced tomatoes

1. Heat a small stockpot over high heat. Pour in the olive oil and let it get hot. Season the shrimp with salt and pepper. Brown the shrimp, about 2 minutes per side. Remove from the pan and set aside. Add the onion, fennel, and garlic, and sauté, stirring occasionally, until the vegetables soften, about 5 minutes. Add the Pernod® and orange juice and bring to a boil. Cook for 2 minutes. Add the tomatoes and bring mixture back to a boil.

2. Season to taste with salt and pepper. Reduce stew to a simmer. Add the shrimp and simmer until they are cooked through, about 4 minutes.

Tools

small stockpot

Grocery List

Fresh

24 very large shrimp
1 large head fennel
2 tomatoes

Packaged

3.15-ounce tube Amore® garlic paste
750 ml bottle Pernod®
10-ounce can frozen orange juice concentrate

Staples

extra-virgin olive oil
onion

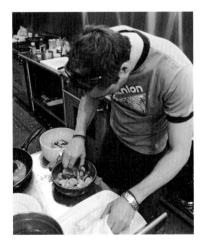

Red Ginger Chicken Satay, page 89

Puffy Chicken with White Beans & Curry, page 82 (above)
Curried Salmon Salad with Avocado Relish, page 144 (right)

Spaghetti and Shrimp with Spring Vegetables, page 175

Crispy Fried Shrimp with Warm Coleslaw, page 165

(right)

Fried Scallops with Melted Onions, page 197

Tuna with Clams, Mushrooms, and Andouille Sausage, recipe page 160 (above)
Seared and Sliced Tuna with Radishes & Snow Peas, recipe page 154 (right)

Sautéed Summer Roll of Salmon with Basil Pesto, recipe page 140

Shrimp and Red Onion Pie, recipe page 173 (above)
Broiled Tuna with Warm Olive & Carrot Vinaigrette, recipe page 149 (right)

Spicy Shrimp
and Bean Stew with Artichokes and Basil

I **used** to walk by the canned and jarred section of the supermarket with an attitude of disdain. I was foolish. Upon closer inspection I've discovered plenty of gems on those shelves. One is marinated artichokes—they really add a lot of flavor and texture to a dish. —R

Tools

large sauté pan

Grocery List

Fresh

1 large zucchini
1½ pounds medium shrimp

Packaged

3.15-ounce tube Amore® garlic paste
25-ounce jar Victoria® Fra Diavolo sauce
8-ounce jar artichoke hearts
10-ounce can green beans
1-ounce package fresh basil

Staples

extra-virgin olive oil
crushed red pepper

1. In a large sauté pan heat the olive oil over medium-high heat. When the oil is hot, add the crushed red pepper and toast for 30 seconds. Add the garlic and zucchini. Season the vegetables with salt and pepper and cook for another minute. Pour in the Fra Diavolo sauce. Cover and bring to a simmer.

2. Season the shrimp with salt and pepper and add to the pan. Add the artichoke hearts and beans to the sauce. Cover and cook an additional 4 to 5 minutes, stirring the stew occasionally to ensure the shrimp cook evenly.

3. When the shrimp are just cooked through, season to taste with salt and pepper. Stir in the basil. Serve stew on a bed of polenta, if desired.

Serves 4

¼ cup Bertolli® extra-virgin olive oil

⅛ teaspoon crushed red pepper

2 tablespoons Amore® garlic paste or 2 large garlic cloves, chopped

1 large zucchini, cut in half the long way and sliced into very thin half moons
Salt and freshly ground pepper

1 25-ounce jar Victoria® Fra Diavolo sauce

1½ pounds medium shrimp, peeled and deveined, tails removed

1 8-ounce jar artichoke hearts packed in olive oil, drained

1 10-ounce can green beans, drained and cut into 1-inch pieces

½ cup chopped fresh basil
Hot cooked instant polenta (optional)

Warm Shrimp and Asparagus Salad with Lemon Mayonnaise

less than 30 minutes

The practice of leaving the tail on a peeled shrimp has always baffled me. Unless it's for shrimp cocktail, the tail does nothing for the dish. I know it makes the shrimp look bigger, but at some point you will have to peel that tail off to eat it. Might as well be now. –R

Serves 4

Salt

Juice and zest of 4 lemons

1¼ cup mayonnaise

1 tablespoon Dijon mustard

Freshly ground pepper

2 bunches pencil-thin asparagus, woody ends trimmed

1½ pounds large shrimp, peeled and deveined, tails removed, and cut in half crosswise down the back

1½ tablespoons Bertolli® extra-virgin olive oil

½ cup fresh basil leaves, torn

1. Bring a large stockpot of water to a rapid boil. Season generously with salt.

2. Meanwhile, in a blender combine the lemon juice, zest, mayonnaise, and mustard. Blend for about 1 minute (this can also be done using a hand-held immersion blender). Season to taste with salt and pepper and refrigerate.

3. Drop the asparagus into the boiling water and cook until almost tender, about 4 minutes. Just before the asparagus is fully cooked, add the shrimp to the stockpot. Cook for about 6 minutes, or until shrimp and asparagus are fully cooked. Drain.

4. In a large bowl, toss the asparagus and shrimp with the olive oil and basil. At this point, you can either stir the lemon mayonnaise into the shrimp and asparagus or serve it in a small bowl on the side.

5. Serve the salad immediately or chill and serve later.

Tools

large stockpot

blender

Grocery List

Fresh

2 bunches pencil-thin asparagus

1½ pounds large shrimp

Packaged

1-ounce package fresh basil

Staples

lemons/mayonnaise

Dijon mustard

extra-virgin olive oil

less than 15
minutes

Mama's Shrimp with Rice and Peppers

My mother dictated this recipe to me over the phone. I watched her make it thousands of times as a kid but I was always too hungry to pay attention to what she was doing. I can't really make any of her recipes as well as she does—and that's exactly as it should be. —R

Tools

large sauté pan

Grocery List

Fresh

3 green peppers
2 pounds medium shrimp, peeled and deveined, tails removed
1 bunch fresh flat-leaf parsley

Packaged

14-ounce box Minute® rice

Staples

unsalted butter
red onion/ chicken broth
crushed red pepper flakes

1. Heat a large sauté pan over high heat. When it's hot add the butter to the pan. Before the butter melts completely add the onion and peppers. Cook, stirring, for about 1 minute. Add the shrimp and rice to the pan. Season with salt and pepper.

2. Cook the shrimp, stirring often, for about 2 minutes. Add the chicken broth and crushed red pepper to the mixture and bring to a boil. Cover and turn heat down to low. Simmer, stirring occasionally, for about 5 more minutes, or until the shrimp are fully cooked.

3. Season to taste with salt and pepper, if necessary. Stir in the parsley and serve.

Serves 4

2	tablespoons unsalted butter
1	large red onion, cut into small chunks
3	green peppers, stemmed and seeded and cut into chunks
2	pounds medium shrimp, peeled and deveined, tails removed
2	cups Minute® rice
	Salt and freshly ground pepper
2	cups chicken broth
¼	teaspoon crushed red pepper flakes
½	bunch fresh flat-leaf parsley, chopped

Tiny Shrimp, Bacon, and Parsnip Casserole

less than 30 minutes

You **never** hear someone asking for small shrimp. In the shrimp world, bigger is better (go figure). I use small shrimp here because they more evenly distribute in a casserole—which means you have a better chance of getting some shrimp in every bite.–R

Serves 4

1   pound bacon, cut into small chunks

4   large parsnips, peeled and grated

    Salt and freshly ground pepper

1   cup heavy cream

1   cup pearl cocktail onions, chopped

1½   pounds small shrimp, peeled and deveined, tails removed

2   tablespoons chopped fresh flat-leaf parsley

1. Preheat the broiler on high.

2. Heat a large sauté pan over high heat. Sauté bacon until cooked through but not too crispy, about 2 minutes. Drain bacon on a paper towel-lined plate. Leave the bacon fat in the pan.

3. Add the parsnips to the pan and turn heat down to medium. Cook, covered, for about 5 to 7 minutes. Season generously with salt and pepper. Add the cream to the pan. Cover and bring to a simmer.

4. Cook until parsnips are completely tender and half of the liquid is reduced, about 5 minutes. Crush the parsnips with a fork or potato masher until mostly smooth, with a few chunks remaining.

5. Stir in the cocktail onions and season to taste with salt and pepper. Spoon the mixture into an 8×8-inch baking dish and spread out evenly. Season the shrimp with salt and pepper. Distribute the shrimp evenly over the parsnip mixture. Broil for 5 to 10 minutes or until shrimp turn opaque. Sprinkle with bacon and parsley and serve immediately.

Tools

large sauté pan

8x8-inch baking dish

Grocery List

Fresh

1 pound bacon
4 large parsnips
1½ pounds small shrimp
1 bunch flat-leaf parsley

Packaged

1 pint heavy cream
8-ounce jar pearl cocktail onions

Staples

less than 15 minutes

Fried Scallops with Melted Onions

In France they call this technique for cooking onions *soubise*. I call it melted. I don't think soubise is a very pretty word (sounds like a fatal disease), but it is pretty to eat. It's a versatile side dish that adds texture and richness to anything it's served with. –R

Tools

medium saucepan

large sauté pan

Grocery List

Fresh

1½ pounds large sea scallops
1 bunch chives

Packaged

14.5-ounce can diced tomatoes

Staples

unsalted butter/corn oil
sweet onions/cornmeal
eggs/lemon

1. Heat a medium saucepan over low heat. Add 3 tablespoons of the butter and onions to the pan and season with salt and pepper. Cover and cook until onions are soft, stirring occasionally, about 15 minutes. Uncover and allow the water to evaporate. Onions should have the texture of marmalade.

2. Meanwhile, in a shallow bowl lightly whisk the egg whites. Spread the cornmeal over a plate. Toss the scallops in the egg whites until they are fully coated. Remove one scallop at a time, allowing the excess egg white to drip off, and dredge in the cornmeal. Shake off excess cornmeal and season with salt and pepper.

3. Heat a large sauté pan over high heat. Add the oil and let it get hot. Carefully place scallops in the pan one at a time and fry until the first side is deep brown and crisped, about 2 minutes. Turn and cook on the second side until the interior is completely opaque and the outside is brown, about 2 minutes. Transfer to a paper towel-lined plate to drain and cover lightly with aluminum foil to keep warm.

4. Drain the oil from the sauté pan and dab clean with a paper towel. Set the pan over medium heat and add the remaining butter. When the milky white solids of the butter have browned, add the tomato and sauté 1 minute. Stir in the lemon juice and chives. Season to taste with salt and pepper.

5. Serve the fried scallops over the melted onions with the tomato-lemon sauce spooned over all.

Serves 4

8 tablespoons unsalted butter (1 stick)
1 pound sweet onions (such as Vidalia or Maui), peeled and sliced thin
Salt and freshly ground pepper
2 egg whites
1 cup fine cornmeal
1½ pounds large sea scallops (U-10 count, preferably)
¼ cup cooking oil
1 cup canned diced tomato
Juice of half a lemon
4 tablespoons chopped fresh chives

See photos, pages 184-185.

Scallops with Mango Relish on Zucchini Cakes

less than 15 minutes

Browning food in hot pans on the stove—the way the scallops are prepared here—or on a hot grill converts their proteins into sugar. It's called caramelizing. Sugar is sweet, and sweet tastes good. –R

Serves 4

½ cup **Bertolli®** extra-virgin olive oil
4 large frozen zucchini cakes or vegetable cakes
1¼ pounds large scallops
    Salt and freshly ground pepper
1½ cups diced ripe mango
1 medium onion, diced
1 jalapeño, finely chopped
    Juice of 1 lime
½ cup chopped fresh cilantro

1. Heat the oil in a very large nonstick sauté pan over medium high heat. Add the zucchini cakes to the oil one at a time. Cook the zucchini cakes until golden brown, about 2 minutes per side. Remove from the pan and place on a cooling rack.

2. Drain all but 2 to 3 tablespoons of the oil from the pan. Heat the pan on high heat until it's very hot. Season the scallops with salt and pepper. Cook the scallops until they are dark brown, about 2 minutes per side.

3. Add the mango, onion, and jalapeño to the pan and continue to cook until the mixture is hot throughout. Stir in the lime juice and cilantro. Season to taste with salt and pepper.

4. Place one zucchini cake on each of four plates. Pile the scallop mixture on top and serve.

Tools

very large nonstick sauté pan

Grocery List

Fresh

1¼ pounds large scallops
2 mangoes
1 jalapeño
1 bunch cilantro

Packaged

2-pound package frozen zucchini cakes

Staples

extra-virgin olive oil
onion
lime

Scallops with Burnt Onions and Lemon Butter

While I am a big fan of browning scallops, there are times when poaching or steaming them is appropriate. Here I have compensated for the sweetness the scallops would have if they were browned by serving them with burnt or charred onions. —R

Tools

large sauté pan

rimmed baking sheet

Grocery List

Fresh

1½ pounds sea scallops
1 bunch chives

Packaged

Staples

lemons
butter
onions

1. Heat a large sauté pan over medium heat. Preheat the broiler.

2. Spread out the onions on a baking sheet. Season generously with salt and pepper. Dot them with ¼ cup of the butter (½ stick) and broil for about 5 minutes or until they're slightly charred and tender.

3. Meanwhile, in the large sauté pan bring the lemon juice and zest to a boil. Add the remaining butter to the pan and allow it to melt. When it comes to a boil, remove from the heat and cool slightly. In a blender (or with an immersion blender), blend the lemon butter on high speed until it's creamy, about 10 seconds.

4. Put the lemon butter back in the sauté pan and let it almost come to a simmer. Season the scallops with salt and pepper and add to pan with lemon butter. Cover and poach scallops for 3 minutes or until just cooked through. (The lemon butter/poaching liquid should never come to a boil while the fish is in it—it should stay just under a simmer.) Stir in the chives.

5. Make a pile of charred onions on each plate and top with scallops. Generously spoon the lemon butter over the top and serve.

Serves 4

4	small red onions, sliced into ⅜-inch-thick rings
	Salt and freshly ground pepper
1¾	cups butter (3½ sticks)
½	cup lemon juice
	Zest from 3 lemons
1½	pounds dry sea scallops, or sea or bay scallops
¼	cup chopped fresh chives

Cooking for the Weekend

So you made it to the weekend, and now you're ready to do something a little more ambitious in the kitchen.

In the spirit of balance, the recipes in this chapter—what I'm calling the "Reserve" recipes—are about cooking as a leisurely pursuit, cooking as entertainment. Maybe you want to impress a date, or your in-laws are in town, or it's a holiday. When these recipes hit the table, people will know immediately that this is not an ordinary meal.
Of course, you don't have to make these dishes alone—in fact—they're not meant to be made alone. One of the most obvious ways to make cooking more fun and easier on yourself is to get your friends involved. Don't invite them over at dinnertime. Invite them over three hours earlier. Maybe some people just want to sit around and sip wine, but somebody is going to want to be a part of the action—and you get a free sous chef. (Incidentally, kids make great sous chefs. There's always something you can get kids to do—clean peas or open packages or set the table. It could be anything.)

The good life is all about enjoying other people's company, and there's no better place to do that than in the kitchen, cooking together.

Top Five Entertaining Tips

When you invite people to your house for dinner, you're making a contract that you're going to make them happy. If people are willing to put their Saturday night in your hands, you better deliver the goods. If you internalize that, every decision is informed by what makes your guests happy.

That's pretty much all you need to know to entertain successfully, but here are a few nuts-and-bolts things I keep in mind when friends are at my table.

Play music—and have it ready to go. The iPod is one of the greatest entertaining devices out there. I have playlists that I know certain friends like. Create those playlists way in advance—and you only have to do it once. It's a set-and-forget thing.

Light with candles only. Candlelight is flattering, it's sexy. Use tons of candles—the cheaper the better because more is better. Not three, maybe a dozen. (No, not a dozen—50.) Put them all around the room—but not on the table (more on why not later).

Skip the centerpiece. It always ends up blocking your view of someone. Same goes for candles. Besides, you can't create anything more beautiful than a bunch of people sitting around a table eating and having fun.

Set a minimalist table. Put only the things you need on the table—a knife, a fork, one plate, one glass (stemless, if possible), wine bottles, and a water pitcher. I don't use bread plates or butter knives, and I don't always use cloth napkins. (I like to use the thicker, square paper napkins or simple hand towels that don't have to be ironed.) Fill each person's glass with wine. When the wine is gone, fill it with water. When the water is gone, pour more wine in it.

Don't worry about formal invitations. Inviting by email or simply calling friends on the phone isn't inappropriate. The simpler you make the whole process, the more often you'll do it. And that's good.

A Word on Wine

I am often asked what's the best salt, what's the best olive oil, what's the best wine. "Best" is so subjective—especially when it comes to wine. I can't tell you what wine you like. If you have a palate and know what you like, that's all that matters.

The vaunted "rules" for pairing wine with food (such as red with red meat, white with fish, etc.) are outdated. I've served red wine with fish, and it was perfect. It has everything to do with the balance of flavors—the sweetness to the acidity, and of course, its weight—and nothing to do with its color.

Now, having brushed aside the old rules, here are some new ones:

You never need to spend more than $15 on a bottle. There are plenty of good, inexpensive wines out there. A high price tag on a wine has to do with how rare it is—it has nothing to do with its intrinsic flavor.

Don't be afraid of screwcap wines. A screwcap is actually the best way to preserve the wine's flavor. Corks may seem more romantic, but they are inefficient.

People tend to like wines from Italy and California. Wine made from the same grape—Merlot, for instance—varies from vintner to vintner, but generally a given varietal will have the same basic characteristics no matter who made it.

For instance, if you like Pinot Grigio from Italy, you're probably going to like Pinot Gris from France because it's made from the same grape. Both Pinot Grigio and Pinot Noir are good, crowd-pleasing wines because they're in the middle of the wine spectrum in terms of weight and flavor.

Wine is food and should be treated as another flavor. The best way to know if a food and a wine go together is to taste them together. It's that simple.

Food and Wine Pairings

Here's a short list of my favorite nationally distributed wines by varietal and brand—all under $20 a bottle—matched with every recipe in the book.

Chardonnay

(California)—Hess Select

Buttermilk-Battered Fried Chicken with Mashed Potatoes and Cabbage, page 86

Chicken-Fried Turkey Steak with Walnut & Ricotta Gravy, page 93

Chicken with Lemon Butter, Thyme & Pimientos, page 84

Marinated Fried Chicken with Herbs, page 55

Warm Chicken & Bacon Salad, page 88

Pork Medallions with Shrimp and Penne Primavera, page 115

Broiled Salmon with Turnip & Onion Relish, page 145

Salmon Cooked in Salt with Sweet & Sour Endive, page 141

Salmon with Crunchy Broccoli & Lemon Butter, page 135

Fried Scallops with Melted Onions, page 197

Scallops with Mango Relish on Zucchini Cakes, page 198

Scallops with Burnt Onions and Lemon Butter, page 199

Tiny Shrimp, Bacon, and Parsnip Casserole, page 196

Broiled Tuna with Warm Olive & Carrot Vinaigrette, page 149

Sweet & Sour Tuna, page 155

Tuna & Tomatoes Poached in Olive Oil, page 159

Tuna Steaks with Red Cabbage Slaw, page 157

Sauvignon Blanc

(France)—Pascal Jolivet Sancerre or Pouilly-Fumé

Beef and Snow Pea Quick Fry, page 37

Boiled Beef and Pappardelle, page 32

Fried Beef with Broccoli and Garlic Sauce, page 38

Chicken Cutlets with Goat Cheese-Scalloped Potatoes, page 51

Chicken Kabobs in Hoisin with Grilled Corn, page 58

Grilled Chicken with Avocado Relish, page 57

Chicken Breasts with Cauliflower and Citrus, page 83

Red Ginger Chicken Satay, page 89

Grilled Pork Chops with Miso & Apple Dressing, page 105

Curried Salmon Salad with Avocado Relish, page 144

Miso Marmalade Salmon with Swiss Chard, page 139

Steamed Salmon in Napa Cabbage, page 142

Crispy Fried Shrimp with Warm Coleslaw, page 165

Jumbo Shrimp and Red Swiss Chard, page 167

Shrimp with Beets and Butter Lettuce, page 170

Sweet & Sticky Coconut Shrimp, page 169 (or a great rum and tonic)

Warm Shrimp and Asparagus Salad with Lemon Mayonnaise, page 194

Crab-Stuffed Tuna with Spinach, page 151

Grilled Tuna Steaks with Sweet & Sour Mangoes, page 150

Cabernet Sauvignon

(California)—Relativity Vineyards

Beef and Potato Gratin, page 42

Beef Pot Roast with Cauliflower and Gravy, page 46

Charred Steak with Mushroom Vinaigrette, page 31

Filet Mignon with Cheese and Potatoes, page 19

Caramelized Lamb Chops with Carrot & Mushroom Stew, page 123

Merlot

(California)—Blackstone

Pork Chops with Turnip Greens, Black-Eyed Peas, and Fresh Cranberry Relish, page 117

Grilled Baby Lamb Chops & Heirloom Tomatoes, page 125

Zinfandel

(California)—Rancho Zabaco

Cold Beef and Italian Bread Salad, page 35

Marmalade-Marinated Flank Steak with Glazed

Carrots, page 24

Roast Beef with Figs and Black Pepper, page 47

Chicken Scaloppine with Potato Pancakes and Port Sauce, page 61

Horseradish-and-Cinnamon-Marinated Skirt Steak with Pears and Scallions, page 23

Sautéed Beef with Spicy Sweet Potato Fries, page 45

Crispy Pork Chops with Rice & Beans, page 118

Pork Burgers with Walnuts and Chow Chow, page 112

Cinnamon-Rubbed Grilled Lamb Chops with Sweet Potatoes, page 131

Grilled Lamb with Sweet and Sour Eggplant, page 126

Syrah

(California)—Francis Ford Coppola Diamond Label Series

Quick Beef and Mushroom Stew, page 34

Sirloin Steak with Kale and Mustard, page 21

Mexican Pork with Okra, page 103

Pinot Noir

(Oregon)—A to Z Wineworks

Beef and Crispy Potatoes with Blue Cheese, page 40

Medallions of Beef with Crab and Squash Stew, page 27

Pork Medallions with Apricot & Endive, page 116

Open-Faced Lamb Sandwich with Cucumber Raita, page 130

Sautéed Summer Roll of Salmon with Basil Pesto, page 140

Tea-Smoked Salmon Fillet with Sweet & Sour Potato Salad, page 138

Shrimp and Red Onion Pie, page 173

Grilled Tuna Steak with Warm Bacon & Green Pea Salad, page 152

Pinot Grigio

(Italy)—Barone Fini

Hot and Sour Beef and Cabbage, page 36

Chicken with Garlic & Spaghetti, page 90

Stuffed Chicken Breasts with Giant White Beans, page 81

Chicken Scaloppine in an Artichoke Broth, page 60

Curried Turkey & Fricassee, page 95

Puffy Chicken with White Beans & Curry, page 82

Turkey Breast with Apricot & Grapefruit Glaze, page 97

Grilled Chicken Breast with Lemon, Pea, and Mint Potatoes, page 56

Grilled Pork Chops with Cumin-Scented Fricassee of Tomatoes, page 111

Curried Salmon with Beet Tartar Salad, page 136

Salmon with Lima Beans & Basil, page 137

Thai Salmon Saté, page 143

Jumbo Shrimp with Hot and Sour Honey Glaze, page 171

Mama's Shrimp with Rice and Peppers, page 195

Shrimp and Cherry Tomatoes, page 166

Shrimp and Fennel Stew, page 176

Shrimp Parmigiano with White Beans and Olives, page 168

Seared & Sliced Tuna with Radishes & Snow Peas, page 154

Grilled Tuna Steaks with Fresh Salsa Verde, page 153 (or good Mexican beer)

Tuna with Lemon, Capers & Parsley, page 158

Valpolicella

(Italy)—Bertani

Grilled Beef Kabobs with Eggplant and Orzo, page 30

Beef Minute Steak with Sour Cherry-Mustard Glaze, page 20

Chicken and Wild Mushroom Marsala, page 52

Creamy Parmesan Risotto with Chicken & Mushrooms, page 91

Turkey & Prosciutto Rolls with Escarole, page 96

Orange and Cinnamon-Glazed Pork Tenderloin, page 101

Pork Chops Puttanesca, page 106

Lamb Chops with Tiny White Beans & Raisins, page 127

Chianti

(Italy)—Fattoria Monsanto

Beef and Fried-Pepper Carpaccio, page 29

Pepper Steak in a Flash, page 22

Chicken & Cauliflower Under a Brick, page 53

Pan-Roasted Chicken Breast with Pickled Peppers, page 64

Fried Pork Cutlets with Chopped Salad, page 102

Shrimp Pappardelle with Smoky Peppers, page 174

Spaghetti and Shrimp with Spring Vegetables, page 175

Tuna and Potatoes alla Mama, page 161

Rosso di Montalcino

(Italy)—Tenuta Carpazo

Beef and Goat Cheese Raviolos, page 44

Ground Beef and Gnocchi, page 43

Chopped Turkey Steaks, Italian Style, page 94

Grilled Stuffed Chicken with Prosciutto and Peppers, page 54

Pork Chops with Potatoes, page 113

Sausage, Peppers & Tomatoes with Fennel Seeds, page 119

Loin Lamb Chops alla Pizzaiolo, page 128

Spicy Shrimp and Bean Stew with Artichokes and Basil, page 193

Tuna & Tomatoes with Creamy Polenta, page 156

Dolcetto

(Italy)—Ceretto

Beef, Miso, and Shiitake Stir Fry, page 39

Beef and Mushroom Chili, page 41

Chipped Beef with Rice Noodles and Chiles, page 33

Medallions of Beef with Gingered Greens, page 26

Tenderloin of Beef with Bacon, Squash, and Five-Spice Powder, page 28

Chicken Breast with Fresh Fig and Arugula Salad, page 59

Shrimp Scampi over Grilled Tomatoes, page 172

Tempranillo

(Spain)—Rioja Viña Izadi

Flank Steak Forestière, page 25

Chicken with Turmeric & Onions, page 85

Quick Chicken Stew with Tomatoes and Mustard, page 87

Grilled Pork with Cherry Tomatoes & Mustard, page 109

Grilled Pork Chops and Peppers alla Brace, page 104

Pork Kabobs with Rosemary-Prune Glaze, page 114

Quick Lamb Stew with Sweet Red Wine Sauce, page 129

Tuna with Clams, Mushrooms & Andouille Sausage, page 160

Côtes du Rhône

(France)—Jaboulet Paralléle 45

Molten Chicken Cutlets with Kale, page 62

Pan-Fried Swiss Chicken Bundles, page 63

Grilled Pork Chops & Beans, page 108

Pork Pot Roast with Artichoke & Peppers, page 107

Pork Chops Stuffed with Portobello Mushrooms, page 110

Curried Grilled Lamb Chops with Chicory, page 124

Grilled Boneless **Sirloin Diane**

This dish was invented in New York in the nineteenth century. It was named after Diana, the Roman goddess of the hunt. Back then, a chef's skills were measured by how well he recreated classic dishes like this one. The creativity we celebrate in chefs today didn't exist then. Now it's fun to go back and reinterpret the classics. I did this at the request of a customer at my restaurant, Union Pacific. –R

Serves 4

- 4 14-ounce prime boneless sirloin steaks, preferably dry aged, trimmed of fat and sinew
- 2 cloves garlic, chopped
- 2 tablespoons Bertolli® extra-virgin olive oil
- 4 tablespoons butter
- 6 ounces portobello mushrooms, stemmed and sliced
- 3½ ounces shiitake mushrooms, stems discarded, sliced
- 3 large shallots, peeled and thinly sliced
- 1 teaspoon chopped fresh thyme
   Salt and freshly ground pepper
- ⅓ cup dry red wine
- ⅓ cup Madeira
- 1 cup heavy cream
- 2 dashes Worcestershire sauce
- 2 tablespoons Dijon mustard
- 1 tablespoon chopped fresh chives
- 2 tablespoons chopped fresh flat-leaf parsley

1. Preheat a grill/grill pan/broiler on high.

2. Rub the steaks with the chopped garlic and coat with the olive oil. Set aside.

3. Meanwhile, heat a large sauté pan over high heat. Add the butter and allow to melt and just start to turn brown. Add the mushrooms, shallots, and thyme. Cook, stirring occasionally, until the mushrooms are slightly golden brown and most of their moisture has evaporated, about 8 to 10 minutes. Season with salt and lots of freshly ground black pepper.

4. Add the red wine and Madeira and cook, stirring, until sauce is reduced by half, about 6 minutes. Turn down the heat to medium and add the heavy cream. Simmer until cream has reduced to sauce consistency, about 4 minutes. Stir in the Worcestershire and mustard.

5. While you are making the sauce, cook the steak. Season the steak generously on both sides with salt and pepper. Grill for about 3½ minutes per side for rare to medium rare. Remove from grill and let the meat rest for about 5 minutes.

6. Slice the sirloin against the grain and arrange on a platter. Add the chives and parsley to the mushroom sauce and season to taste with salt and pepper if necessary. Spoon the sauce over the steak and serve.

wine **California Syrah** Big fruit, medium tannins (About $13 to $15)

Slow-Roasted Leg of Lamb

No one has time to cook slow—but that doesn't mean we shouldn't try to make the time every once in a while. The slower and more gently you cook any food, the more moist, tender, and flavorful it comes out, and it doesn't require the kind of supervision that quick cooking does. As late-night television pitchman Ron Popeil says, "Set it and forget it." –R

1. Trim lamb of about 2 tablespoons of fat.

2. Place the fat in a food processor with garlic, rosemary, sage, 1½ tablespoons salt, olive oil, black pepper, and crushed red pepper. Puree until almost smooth. Rub mixture over entire surface of lamb. Cover and marinate in the refrigerator overnight.

3. Preheat oven to 300°F. Place lamb on a roasting rack in a roasting pan. Roast in the oven for 4 to 5 hours, or until the internal temperature reaches 140°F, for a slightly pink medium doneness. (That's perfect for lamb. Too rare, and it's tough. Too well done, and it's dry. However, I'd rather have it too well done than too rare.)

4. Allow lamb to rest about 15 minutes. Slice and serve warm.

wine **Cabernet Sauvignon from California or Washington State.** Lots of fruit and great tannic structure will complement the full flavors of the roasted lamb and garlic. (About $15 to $18)

Serves 6 to 8

1	7-pound bone-in leg of lamb
7	garlic cloves, peeled
¼	cup fresh rosemary
10	fresh sage leaves
1½	tablespoons salt, plus more for seasoning
⅓	cup Bertolli® extra-virgin olive oil
1	teaspoon freshly ground pepper
¼	teaspoon crushed red pepper flakes

Meatloaf with Fried Onions and Tomato Gravy

I once thought that the mix my mother uses to make meatballs would make a great meatloaf, so I experimented and came up with this hunger-killing dish. I didn't want to use the same tomato sauce, so I adapted it and made a tomato gravy with fried onions. When you're serving this, be sure to first top the meatloaf with the gravy—then the onions. —R

Meatloaf

Serves 6 to 8

- Aluminum foil
- Nonstick cooking spray
- 2½ pounds ground beef
- 2½ pounds ground pork
- 1 15-ounce container Progresso® Italian-style breadcrumbs
- 10 eggs, beaten
- ½ cup water
- ½ cup finely grated Parmigiano-Reggiano cheese
- 1 cup chopped fresh flat-leaf parsley

Tomato Gravy

- 2 tablespoons butter
- 4 garlic cloves, smashed
- 2 tablespoons tomato paste
- 2 tablespoons all-purpose flour
- 2 14-ounce cans chicken broth
- ¼ cup red wine vinegar
- 1 28-ounce can plum tomatoes, plus juices, chopped
- 1 tablespoon dried oregano
- Salt and freshly ground pepper

Meatloaf

1. Preheat oven to 350°F.

2. Line a large, rimmed baking sheet with aluminum foil and spray with cooking spray.

3. In a large bowl, combine beef, pork, breadcrumbs, eggs, water, cheese, and parsley. Using your hands (it's the best way), mix until all of the ingredients are well combined. Form into a loaf shape and place on the prepared baking sheet.

4. Bake for 45 minutes, or until meatloaf has an internal temperature of 160°F.

Tomato Gravy

1. In a large saucepan heat butter over medium-high heat. Allow butter to foam and begin to brown. Add the smashed garlic and brown slightly, about 2 minutes. Add tomato paste and cook, stirring occasionally, until it is a deep brick red, about 3 to 5 minutes. Sprinkle in flour and cook, stirring constantly, for 1 to 2 minutes. Whisk in the chicken broth. Cook, stirring constantly with a wooden spoon, for 10 to 12 minutes, or until mixture is golden brown.

Fried Onions

2   quarts cooking oil, for frying

3   large Spanish onions, peeled, cut in half, and sliced thinly

4   cups milk

4   cups all purpose-flour

     Salt and freshly ground pepper

See photo, page 80.

2. Add the vinegar and the tomatoes and their juices, crushing them with your hands as you add them to the pan. Simmer, uncovered, for 30 minutes. Stir in the dried oregano and season to taste with salt and pepper. Serve atop the meatloaf.

Fried Onions

1. In a very large, heavy-bottomed stockpot, heat the oil to 350°F.

2. Soak the onions in the milk for at least 10 minutes. Season flour to taste with salt and pepper. When oil is hot, drain onions and dredge them in the seasoned flour, making sure to remove excess flour.

3. Divide the onions into three batches. Fry the onions in the hot oil one batch at a time until extremely golden brown and crispy, about 3 to 5 minutes. Remove from pot with a small strainer or slotted spoon and drain on a paper towel-lined platter or baking pan. Serve on top of dressed meatloaf.

wine California Merlot Good fruit, medium tannin; stands up to the protein and fat in the meatloaf (About $12)

Fennel Stuffed **Loin of Pork**

This dish was created for my appearance on *The Martha Stewart Show*. Butterflying is a technique for splitting poultry, beef, pork, or seafood horizontally without cutting all the way through. When opened up, the food resembles a butterfly shape. The result is a uniform thickness that cooks evenly. —R

Serves 6 to 8

- ⅓ cup light miso
- ½ cup freshly squeezed lemon juice, plus juice of 1 lemon
- 1 cup orange marmalade
  Coarse salt and freshly ground pepper
- 1 3-pound boneless pork loin, shoulder end, trimmed and butterflied
- 1 tablespoon Bertolli® extra-virgin olive oil, plus more for rubbing
- ¼ pound slab bacon, rind removed, cut into ½-inch pieces

- 1 medium bulb fennel, trimmed and cut into ¼-inch pieces
- 1 medium yellow onion, cut into ¼-inch pieces
- 2 sprigs fresh tarragon
- 1 garlic clove, finely chopped
- 3 tablespoons sugar
- 3 tablespoons Martini & Rossi® rosso vermouth
- ¼ teaspoon crushed red pepper flakes
- ¼ teaspoon fennel seeds, crushed
  Zest of 1 orange
  Butcher's twine

1. Preheat oven to 475°F.

2. In a large shallow baking dish, stir together miso, the ½ cup lemon juice, and marmalade. Season to taste with salt and pepper. Set aside ½ cup of the glaze mixture. Add pork to dish, turning to coat. Marinate at room temperature for 15 minutes.

3. Heat a large skillet over high heat. Add the olive oil and bacon. Cook the bacon, stirring occasionally, until fat is rendered, about 3 minutes. Add fennel and onion. Cook, stirring occasionally, until fennel begins to soften, about 10 minutes. Add the tarragon and garlic; cook for 2 minutes. Drain excess fat, if necessary, and discard tarragon. Add sugar and cook, stirring, until dissolved. Add the vermouth, and using a wooden spoon, scrape up any browned bits. Cook until nearly all of the liquid has evaporated, about 5 minutes. Add remaining juice of 1 lemon, crushed red pepper, and fennel seeds. Cook until liquid has evaporated. Remove from heat and toss with zest. Set aside.

How to Butterfly

Although I suggest that you have your butcher butterfly this roast for you, it doesn't hurt to learn this technique.

Beginning on the thicker side of whatever you're butterflying, hold a sharp knife parallel to the cutting surface and slice the food almost completely in half without cutting all the way through. After you butterfly the food, open it up and flatten it; you may have to pound it to an even thickness.

To pound and flatten it, place the food between two pieces of plastic wrap. Using a meat mallet or the back of a pan, pound the food until it is even throughout—and be careful not to tear it.

What to Butterfly

You can butterfly most meats, poultry, fish, and shellfish. Examples include chicken, leg of lamb, pork roast, Cornish hen, flank steak, and large shrimp. Butterflied foods such as pork roast and leg of lamb are perfect for stuffing.

4. Remove pork from marinade. Pat dry with a paper towel and discard marinade. Place pork on a work surface, cut side up. Season with salt and pepper. Evenly spread fennel mixture over pork. Starting at the long end, roll up the pork. Using butcher's twine, tie the pork every 1½ to 2 inches.

5. Place the pork in a roasting pan fitted with a rack. Rub the pork with some olive oil and season with salt and pepper. Roast the pork until browned, about 20 to 25 minutes. Reduce heat to 350°F and continue roasting until an instant-read thermometer inserted into the thickest part registers 130°F degrees, about 15 to 20 minutes. (Cover with foil if it's browning too quickly.)

6. Increase the oven temperature to 550°F. If the pork is covered, uncover it. Brush with reserved glaze. Continue to roast until dark brown, about 5 to 8 minutes.

7. Transfer the pork to a serving platter. Cover lightly with foil and let rest for 10 to 20 minutes. Slice pork into ¼-inch-thick pieces and serve.

wine **Cotes du Rhone Red from France** Fruit, earthiness, not too much tannin (About $13)

Perfect Roasted **Chicken**
Smothered in Caramelized Onions

The secret to roast chicken is not to overcook it. It's true that a bird is fully cooked when it reaches an internal temperature of 160°F. Fully cooked means there are no juices left and any fat (fat is flavor) has been rendered out. That's not what you want. The idea is to remove the bird from the oven when it reaches 145°F. It will continue to cook as it rests and will wind up on your plate at no more than 160°F. Perfect. —R

Serves 4

1	3- to 4-pound roasting chicken
	Salt and freshly ground pepper
6	tablespoons butter
4	large Vidalia onions, peeled and thinly sliced
1½	tablespoons fresh thyme leaves

See photo, page 73.

1. Preheat oven to 350°F.

2. Season chicken all over with salt and pepper. Season the cavity with twice as much salt and pepper as on the outside. Place chicken on a roasting rack in a roasting pan and roast in the oven for about 55 to 60 minutes. Check the temperature every 10 minutes after a half hour of roasting. Insert the thermometer in the thickest part of the thigh. If it reaches 130°F to 140°F before 55 minutes, then turn up the oven sooner than this recipe indicates.

3. Once the thermometer says 135°F to 140°F, turn the oven temperature up to 500°F and continue roasting the chicken for another 15 to 25 minutes, or until the skin is a deep golden brown and crisp and the flesh is just cooked through, about 145°F to 150°F.

4. Remove from oven and allow to rest for about 10 to 15 minutes before cutting. This is a very important step. If you don't wait, all the juices will run out after the first slice.

5. While the chicken is roasting, heat a large sauté pan over medium heat. Melt the butter and add the onions and thyme leaves. Cook, stirring occasionally, until the onions become tender, about 25 minutes. When they begin to caramelize, turn the heat down slightly and continue to cook, stirring frequently, so that they caramelize evenly but do not burn. If they start to burn, gradually turn the heat down. Toward the end of the cooking process, season the onions with salt and pepper to taste. The whole process should take about 30 minutes.

6. When the chicken has rested, break it down into 2 breasts, 2 drumsticks, 2 thighs, and 2 wings and arrange them on a platter. Smother the chicken with the onions and serve.

wine California Chardonnay, but one that is oak-aged and buttery. Oak flavor will beautifully complement the flavors of the chicken and the onions. (About $15)

No-Brainer Holiday **Duck**

Everyone thinks of duck as being so fussy and fancy, but it's not. This one cooks very slowly—4 hours—to give you lots of time to prep the other ingredients (which aren't hard, either). –R

Duck
Serves 4

1 white Peking duck, trussed by the butcher
   Salt and freshly ground pepper
   Quince and Grenadine Lacquer, recipe at right
   Sweet and Sour Red Cabbage, recipe page 217

Quince and Grenadine Lacquer
Makes enough to glaze one duck

8 quince
2 tablespoons grenadine
1½ teaspoons lemon juice

1. Preheat the oven to 275°F.

2. Season the duck with salt and pepper. Using the tines of a fork, prick the skin of the duck all over. Place the duck on a rack in a roasting pan and pour about 3 inches of water into the bottom of the pan. This will prevent the oven from smoking when the fat renders off the duck. Set the pan in the oven and cook for 4 hours. Every half hour or so, prick the duck again with a fork (the holes will close up as the duck cooks). If the water level gets too low, add hot water to the pan.

3. After 4 hours, remove the duck from the oven and increase the heat to 500°F. When the oven is ready, put the duck back in and cook until the skin turns golden brown and crispy, about 10 minutes. Remove from the oven. Let rest 2 or 3 minutes, then glaze with Quince and Grenadine Lacquer and carve.

wine **California Zinfandel** Spicy, earthy, berry flavors will stand up to the gaminess of the duck. (About $15)

Quince and Grenadine Lacquer

1. Peel the quince and put the peels in a small saucepan. Cover with about 3 cups of water and bring to a boil; boil 2 minutes. Strain and set aside.

Sweet and Sour Red Cabbage

1	tablespoon cooking oil		Salt and freshly ground black pepper
4	ounces bacon, cut in thin strips	¼	cup honey
2	onions, peeled, halved, and thinly sliced	½	cup red wine vinegar
3	garlic cloves, minced	3	cups chicken broth
2	medium heads red cabbage, cored, and thinly sliced	1	tablespoon caraway seeds

2. Core and dice the quince and put the flesh in a blender. Puree with the grenadine and enough of the peel water to make a smooth puree, about 2 cups. Pour through a fine-mesh strainer into a clean saucepan. Bring to a low simmer over medium heat and reduce it slowly until thickened to a glaze-like consistency, about 30 to 40 minutes. Season to taste with the lemon juice.

3. When ready to serve, warm the glaze up until it is pourable. Using a wide pastry brush or spatula, coat the duck with the glaze before carving.

Sweet and Sour Red Cabbage

1. In a large sauté pan heat the oil over medium heat. Add bacon and cook until the bacon has rendered its fat but is not crispy, about 3 minutes. Add the onions and garlic and cook, stirring occasionally, until the vegetables are completely soft and beginning to brown, about 8 minutes. Add the cabbage to the pan and stir well. Season with salt and pepper and cook for another 2 to 3 minutes, or until the cabbage begins to wilt.

2. Add the honey and stir to coat the cabbage. Continue to cook until the cabbage is tender and has released most of its liquid, about 12 minutes. Add the vinegar and cook until liquid has reduced by half, about 3 minutes. Add enough chicken broth to come halfway up the cabbage and lower the heat so it just simmers. Cover and cook 30 minutes or until the cabbage is completely tender throughout. Add the caraway to the cabbage and stir well before serving with the duck.

John Dory with a Ragout of Dill and
Littleneck Clams

The story of John Dory is full of religious symbolism. The fish was originally called St. Pierre, as in Saint Peter, the disciple of Jesus who became the first pope. It has two large brown spots on either side of its head. These are said to be St. Peter's thumb and forefinger—the print left from when he picked the fish out of the water during the performance of a miracle. There's another miracle here: the wondrous flavor and texture of the fish. —R

Serves 4

4   pounds littleneck, Manila, or other small clams
2   tablespoons cornmeal
¼   cup salt for blanching, plus more for seasoning
½   cup fresh flat-leaf parsley
½   bunch dill
1   cup dry white wine

2   tablespoons chopped shallots
2   tablespoons cooking oil
3   tablespoons butter
4   6-ounce skinless John Dory (also "St. Pierre"), cod, grouper, or red snapper fillets
    Salt and freshly ground black pepper
    Wondra® flour
    Luxurious Potato Purée (see recipe, page 220)

1. Place clams in a large bowl, cover with cold water, add cornmeal, and gently shake the bowl. Let stand for 1 hour. "Chipping" clams gets them to purge any sand. At the end of the hour, you should see sand at the bottom of the bowl. Remove from water and hold in the refrigerator.

2. Bring a medium saucepan of water to a boil and add 2 tablespoons of the salt. While water comes to a boil, prepare an ice bath with 2 tablespoons salt dissolved into water. Blanch the parsley in boiling water for 30 seconds and immediately submerge in ice bath. Let sit for 1 minute, then remove with a slotted spoon (don't drain ice bath).

When hot water has returned to a rolling boil, add dill and blanch 5 seconds. Shock dill in same ice bath for 1 minute. Pack blanched parsley and dill in a blender with ⅓ cup cold water. Puree herbs, pouring in more water as needed through the blender's feedhole until blade turns freely. Puree until smooth. Hold aside.

3. Heat a very large sauté pan with a tight-fitting lid (a see-through glass cover will let you watch the clams opening) over medium-high heat and add wine and shallots. When mixture comes to a boil, arrange clams in a single layer so that all have contact with the bottom of the pan; work in batches if necessary. Cover the pan and steam the clams, pulling each from the pan as soon as its shell is opened wide. All clams should open within 10 minutes. Discard

any clams that haven't opened. Shake liquid out of clams into the steaming broth, spread clams on a baking sheet, and refrigerate for 30 minutes. Wipe the pan clean with a paper towel. Strain the broth through a fine-mesh sieve and return it to the clean pan.

4. After clams have been refrigerated, you may remove them from their shells. (A simpler and charmingly rustic approach is to serve them in their shells—the choice is yours.)

5. Heat the oil and 2 tablespoons of the butter over high heat in another large sauté pan. Season the fillets with salt and pepper on one side only. Dust the same side with the Wondra® flour. When the butter and oil starts to foam and smoke, place fish dusted-side-down in the pan and cook until golden brown, 1 to 2 minutes. Blot moisture from tops of fillets, repeat seasoning (salt, pepper, Wondra® flour), and flip. Cook on the second side 1 to 2 minutes. Transfer fillets to a paper towel-lined plate. Cover lightly with foil to keep warm.

6. Turn heat to medium-low under the pan containing the strained clam cooking liquid. Add the parsley-dill puree, stir, and heat until sauce is warmed through, about 3 minutes. Add the remaining 1 tablespoon butter and swirl pan to incorporate butter. Season to taste with salt and pepper. Remove pan from heat. Add clams, in their shells or shelled, to sauce and swirl pan to coat.

7. Place a round of Luxurious Potato Purée (see page 220) on each plate and center a fillet on the potatoes. Ladle the clam sauce over entire dish. Serve hot.

wine **Non-oaked French Chardonnay from Burgundy, Macon, Pouilly-Fuisse, or Chablis** Oaky, woody wines are best for drinking as a cocktail; lighter white wines like these are a nice balance to the delicate flavor of the fish. (About $13 to $18)

Luxurious **Potato Purée**

Like any luxury, this dish is meant for special occasions only. You might want to get a pass from your cardiologist before taking a bite. It's all about the butter—the more, the better. —R

Serves 6

- 4 pounds waxy potatoes such as Yukon golds or fingerlings, peeled and cut into ½-inch rounds
- 3 tablespoons salt
- 12 tablespoons unsalted butter (1½ sticks)
- ½ cup whole milk
  Freshly ground pepper
  Ground nutmeg

1. Place potatoes in a large stockpot and fill with water to cover potatoes by 2 inches. Add salt. Bring to a boil and lower heat immediately so water is at a brisk simmer. (The potatoes will break up if they're boiled, resulting in smaller pieces of potato that cook too fast, absorb too much water, and become mushy.) Simmer for about 20 minutes or until they are easily pierced with a knife. Drain the potatoes. Immediately pass them through the fine disk of a food mill or a potato ricer, letting the potatoes fall into a clean stockpot. (You can also mash the potatoes with a potato masher, but the final texture of the purée won't be as refined.)

2. Place pot with mashed potatoes over low heat. Add butter 2 tablespoons at a time, mixing vigorously with a rubber spatula. When all the butter has been incorporated, add the milk and stir to combine. Season to taste with pepper, nutmeg, and more salt, if desired.

Soft Shell Crabs with XO Sauce

When we discovered XO sauce—a Chinese condiment made with dried shrimp, dried scallops, red chiles, shallots, garlic, oyster extract, shrimp roe, sugar, salt, and seasonings—it went through the kitchens of New Yo City restaurants faster than the pictures of the New York Times restaura critic. It has incredible flavor and a name that looks great on a menu. —R

1. In a small bowl beat 2 eggs with a whisk or fork. Brush crabs on both sides with egg. Place cornmeal in a bowl and dredge crabs in cornmeal.

2. Pour 1 inch of cooking oil into a large sauté pan—cast iron if possible—and place pan over high heat. When oil is very hot, add as many crabs as will fit in the pan and still leave a third of the skillet space free. Season crabs with salt and pepper. Sauté until crispy and browned, about 2 minutes per side. Remove from pan and drain and place on a paper towel-lined plate. Cook remaining crabs. Keep cooked crabs warm by tenting with aluminum foil.

3. Wipe the skillet with a paper towel to remove any cornmeal, but leave a thin film of oil in the pan. Return to high heat. Add the scallions, season with salt and pepper to taste, and sauté, stirring continuously, until wilted and lightly browned, about 4 minutes. Add the XO sauce, lemon juice, and mirin; stir to combine for 1 minute. Reduce heat to medium. Beat remaining 4 eggs in a bowl. Pour eggs over scallion mixture, leave undisturbed for 10 seconds, then stir eggs to break, cooking eggs no more than 1 minute total. Eggs should be loosely set.

4. Place 2 crabs on each plate and smother with the egg-scallion-XO sauce. Serve hot.

wine **German Riesling** Sweetness complements the flavors in the XO sauce. (About $10 to $13)

Serves 4

6 eggs
8 jumbo live soft-shell crabs, cleaned by your fishmonger
1 cup fine cornmeal
   Cooking oil
   Salt and freshly ground black pepper
8 scallions, root ends trimmed and halved lengthwise
1 tablespoon Chinese XO sauce (available in Chinese groceries)
¼ cup lemon juice
1 tablespoon mirin

Clams with Scallions, Nori, and Sesame

In Japan there is a condiment called *Furikake*, or rice seasoning. The ingredients are the toasted sesame seeds and flakes of toasted nori (Japanese seaweed paper for sushi making) I talk about below. You can make your own, but very good quality blends are sold in Asian markets and even in some Western markets. —R

Serves 4

- 24 littleneck or cherrystone clams, in their shells
- 2 tablespoons cornmeal
- ½ sheet sushi nori (square-shape seaweed used to roll sushi)
- 2 teaspoons sesame seeds
- 3 bunches scallions, roots trimmed, white and pale green sections cut into 2-inch lengths, plus 2 tablespoons finely chopped dark green scallion tops
- 2 tablespoons light soy sauce or ½ teaspoon regular soy sauce
- 5 tablespoons rice wine vinegar
- ¼ cup mirin
- 1½ cups water
  Several drops Bertolli® extra-virgin olive oil

1. Place clams in a large bowl, cover with cold water, add cornmeal, and gently shake the bowl. Let stand for 1 hour. At the end of the hour, you should see sand at the bottom of the bowl.

2. Light a gas burner or heat an electric burner on high. Lightly grasp the nori sheet with tongs and pass quickly several times through the flame or over the burner, stopping when it gives off a faint toasted seaweed scent. It should not change in form or color. Coarsely chop nori and set aside.

3. Heat a small sauté pan over medium-low heat and add sesame seeds. Toast the seeds, shaking pan frequently, just until fragrant and golden brown, about 3 to 5 minutes. In a spice grinder or mortar with pestle, grind nori and sesame seeds together until roughly crushed. Transfer to a small bowl and stir in chopped dark green scallions.

4. In a large sauté pan, combine the soy sauce, vinegar, mirin, and water. Bring to a simmer and add the 2-inch scallion pieces. Cook until tender, about 3 minutes. Add the clams to stockpot, cover, and cook just until all the clam shells have opened, about 8 minutes. Stir midway so that clams buried at the bottom get an equal shot of steam. Discard any clams that do not open.

5. Add nori-scallion mixture to the pot. Put 6 clams in each of four shallow bowls. Ladle broth into the bowls and add a few drops of olive oil.

wine **New Zealand Sauvignon Blanc** Slightly sweet, to match the nori with the sesame (About $12)

Linguini with Clams

Cherrystone clams are a medium-size (usually about 2½ inches across) East Coast hard-shell clam. When you're buying fresh clams—and again before you cook them—be sure they're OK to eat. (Try to cook them the same day you buy them.) Check to see that the shells are tightly closed. If a shell is slightly open, tap it gently. If it doesn't close up, the clam is dead and should be tossed. −R

1. Strain liquor from the clams (the liquid inside the shells) into a bowl through a mesh strainer lined with a cheesecloth. Slice the clams into two or three pieces and place in the clam liquor.

2. Heat a large sauté pan over high heat. When it's hot, add the oil. When the oil is hot, add the garlic and crushed red pepper. Cook and stir until the garlic is a light golden color, about 1 to 2 minutes.

3. Add the clams with all of their liquor and cook, stirring occasionally, for about 2 minutes.

4. Cook the pasta according to package directions. Drain, reserving about 1 cup of the pasta-cooking liquid. Add the pasta to the sauté pan with about 3 tablespoons of the pasta-cooking water. Stir well to combine. Garnish with parsley. Season to taste with salt and pepper and serve.

wine An Italian white such as Soave, Pinot Grigio, or Gavi Fruit and crisp acidity key—acidity helps cut the richness of the clam sauce (About $8 to $13)

Serves 4

1 pound fresh cherrystone clams, shucked with juice
3 tablespoons Bertolli® extra-virgin olive oil
2 tablespoons chopped garlic
1 teaspoon crushed red pepper
1 pound dried linguini
2 tablespoons chopped fresh flat-leaf parsley
Salt and freshly ground black pepper

Gnocchi with Veal and Porcini Ragu

San Marzano tomatoes are considered the king of plum tomatoes. They grow in the mineral-rich volcanic soil around a small town of the same name near Naples, Italy. They're extra juicy, with firm, rich flesh and fabulous flavor and fragrance. In fact, they're the only tomatoes that can be used on true Neapolitan pizza. They are truly worth seeking out. —R

Serves 6

1 cup water	½ cup dry red wine
1 ounce dried porcini mushrooms	3 cups chicken broth
¼ cup Bertolli® extra-virgin olive oil	1 28-ounce can whole San Marzano tomatoes, crushed by hand, plus juices
1 small onion, finely chopped	2 fresh bay leaves
¼ cup fresh fennel, chopped	2 teaspoons chopped fresh sage
1 small carrot, peeled and finely chopped	6 large Idaho potatoes, scrubbed
¼ cup minced fresh flat-leaf parsley	2 large eggs
2 garlic cloves, minced	2 teaspoons salt, plus more for cooking water and seasoning
½ pound veal stew meat, chopped	
½ pound ground veal meat	

1. In a small saucepan bring 1 cup of water and the mushrooms to a boil. Remove from the heat and let stand 15 minutes. Strain the soaking liquid through a coffee filter into a bowl. Coarsely chop mushrooms. Set mushrooms and soaking liquid aside separately.

2. Heat the olive oil in a large, heavy-bottomed skillet over medium-high heat. Add onion, fennel, carrot, parsley, and garlic. Cook, stirring occasionally, until vegetables are tender, about 10 minutes. Remove vegetables and set aside.

3. Add the veal stew meat and ground veal to the pan and cook, stirring, until all sides are browned, about 8 to 10 minutes. Add the wine to the pan. Increase the heat to high and cook, stirring occasionally, until the liquid is cooked off, about 5 minutes. Add the cooked vegetables, chicken broth, tomatoes and juices, and reserved mushroom-soaking liquid. Turn heat down and simmer until most of the liquid is absorbed, about 45 minutes. Add bay leaves, sage, and mushrooms. Simmer, uncovered, stirring occasionally, until sauce thickens, about 1 to 2 hours.

½ teaspoon freshly ground pepper, plus more for
    seasoning
    Pinch of ground nutmeg
½ cup grated Parmigiano-Reggiano cheese
4   cups unbleached all-purpose flour

4. Meanwhile, in a large saucepan or Dutch oven boil the potatoes in salted water until they are easily pierced with a fork, about 25 minutes. Drain. When the potatoes are cool enough to handle but still hot, peel them using a tea towel. Let stand just until cool. Press potatoes through a ricer or food mill. Spread on the counter and let cool.

5. In a small bowl beat the eggs, the 2 teaspoons salt, pepper, and nutmeg. Gather the potatoes in a mound and form a well in the center. Pour the egg mixture into the well. Knead the potato and egg mixture together, gradually adding in the cheese. Add enough of the flour to form a smooth but slightly sticky dough. (Don't overknead, or your gnocchi will be heavy.) Cover the dough with a damp clean kitchen towel or plastic wrap and set aside.

6. When the sauce is almost done, bring a large stockpot of water to boil. Add a sprinkle of salt. Pull off little pieces of the dough and drop into the boiling water. Cook until gnocchi rise to the surface. (You'll have to cook gnocchi in batches.) Remove with a slotted spoon and keep warm until serving time.

7. Season sauce to taste with salt and pepper. Serve over gnocchi.

wine **Aglianico from Campania or anywhere in Southern Italy** Bold, robust fruit with big flavor (About $15)

Spaghetti Scarpariello

I met my friend Antonio Pisaniello in southern Italy when I was on a research trip, eating my way through the south to find the best food and inspiration. Of the 100-plus restaurants I ate in on that trip, Antonio's cooked the best meal of all, and it included this dish. —R

Serves 4

- 1 pound dried spaghetti
  Salt
- ¼ cup Bertolli® extra-virgin olive oil
- 6 garlic cloves, peeled and thinly sliced
- 5 oil-packed anchovy fillets
- 1 28-ounce canned plum tomatoes, chopped
- 1 teaspoon anchovy paste
- 1 sprig fresh oregano
- ½ cup fine plain breadcrumbs
- 1 tablespoon capers
- ½ cup quartered black olives
  Pinch of crushed red pepper flakes
  Salt and freshly ground pepper

1. Cook the spaghetti according to package instructions, with the exception of stirring the spaghetti constantly for the first 2 minutes after adding it to the (heavily) salted boiling water. Drain, reserving ½ cup of the cooking water.

2. In a large skillet over medium heat, warm the olive oil, then add the garlic. Cook and stir until the garlic turns light golden brown. Add the anchovies, breaking them up with the edge of a spoon. Add the tomatoes, anchovy paste, and oregano. Simmer, stirring constantly, about 3 minutes.

3. Add the breadcrumbs, capers, olives, and crushed red pepper. Add the cooked pasta to the skillet, along with enough of the reserved cooking water to make a glossy, loose sauce. Toss nonstop for about 2 minutes and serve.

wine **Chianti** Lots of aromatic fruit, low tannin, and great acidity are a perfect foil for the capers, anchovies, and olives. (About $10 to $15)

Pappardelle with Portobellos and Pecorino

Pecorino is a sharp, salty Italian cheese made from sheep's milk. Like Parmiganio-Reggiano, it is a "grana," or hard, granular cheese that's perfect for grating. There are several varieties, but the most commonly available is pecorino romano. It's a more affordable alternative to Parmigiano-Reggiano—especially fortuitous if you like that pungent taste. —R

1. Cook pasta according to package directions.

2. Meanwhile, heat oil in a large sauté pan over medium-high heat until hot. Add the mushrooms and cook, stirring occasionally, until mushrooms are tender, about 6 minutes.

3. Add the garlic and sauté for another minute or until fragrant. Season to taste with salt and lots of pepper. Add the vermouth and bring to a simmer. Add the butter to the pan and swirl to blend. Continue to cook until the sauce is reduced by about half, about 3 minutes.

4. In a large (preferably warm) bowl, toss pasta with the mushroom sauce, parsley, and cheese. Season to taste with salt and pepper and serve.

wine Tempranillo from Spain, from Rioja, or Ribera del Duero Great intensity of flavor with fruit and spiciness will stand up to the strong flavors of the mushrooms and cheese. (About $15)

Serves 4

- 12 ounces dried pappardelle pasta
- 3 tablespoons Bertolli® extra-virgin olive oil
- 1 pound portobello mushrooms, stemmed and sliced
- 3 large garlic cloves, chopped
  Salt and coarsely ground pepper
- ⅔ cup Martini & Rossi® extra-dry vermouth
- 8 tablespoons butter (1 stick), cut into chunks
- ½ cup fresh flat-leaf parsley, chopped
- 1 cup freshly grated pecorino cheese

Tubettini Artichoke **Bolognese**

If you ask an Italian if there was such a thing as Artichoke Bolognese, you might get a sneer. I love artichokes and think that chopping them into a sauce similar to a bolognese is a really good idea. It tastes great and coats the pasta beautifully. –R

For the pasta

Serves 6 to 8

1½	pounds dried tubettini pasta
½	cup grated ricotta salata cheese

For the artichokes

6	large artichokes
⅓	cup Bertolli® extra-virgin olive oil
½	pound pancetta
½	cup fresh parsley
½	bunch fresh thyme
½	cup fresh basil
5	fresh mint leaves
¼	bunch fresh sage
2	sprigs fresh rosemary
	Cheesecloth
	Butcher's twine
5	garlic cloves, sliced

Artichokes

1. Trim, halve, and core the artichokes down to the heart.

2. In a large saucepan heat the ⅓ cup olive oil over medium heat. Add the pancetta. Cook, stirring occasionally, for 5 minutes. Make a sachet by placing the parsley, thyme, basil, mint, sage, and rosemary in the center of a double-thick 6-inch square of cotton cheesecloth. Tie closed with a clean piece of butcher's twine, leaving a long end to help pull it out later. Add the sachet along with the garlic to the pancetta. Add chile, coriander, peppercorn, bay leaf, and turmeric and cook until spices begin to pop.

3. Add artichokes, wine, the ½ cup olive oil, and enough water to cover the artichokes. Cover pan with parchment paper and simmer until artichokes are not quite cooked, about 30 minutes. Strain the artichoke cooking liquid and save it. Finely chop artichokes and set aside.

Sauce

1. Heat a large saucepan pan over high heat. Add the ¼ cup oil and let it get hot. Add the sausage. Cook, stirring occasionally, until sausage is golden brown, about 7 to 9 minutes. Remove the sausage from the pan and set aside. Remove all but 5 tablespoons of oil from the pan. Put the pan back over medium-high heat. Add the onion and the garlic. Cook

1	dried red chile
1	tablespoon coriander seeds
1	tablespoon black peppercorns
1	fresh bay leaf
3	teaspoons ground turmeric
2	cups dry white wine
½	cup Bertolli® extra-virgin olive oil
	Water
	Parchment paper

For the sauce

¼	cup Bertolli® extra-virgin olive oil
1	pound sweet Italian pork sausage links, chopped
1	large Vidalia onion, chopped
6	garlic cloves, chopped
2	tablespoons tomato paste
1	28-ounce can crushed tomatoes
1	tablespoon crushed red pepper
1	cup heavy cream

the vegetables, stirring occasionally, for about 8 minutes or until they are translucent and tender. Add the tomato paste, crushed tomatoes, cooked sausage, and crushed red pepper. Turn heat down to low and simmer for about 1 hour.

2. When sauce is almost done cooking, cook the pasta according to package instructions.

3. Add the chopped artichokes to the sauce and stir in the cream. Serve over cooked tubetti pasta with grated ricotta salata sprinkled on top.

wine Valpolicella from Italy (Veneto region) Richness of the three grapes of Valpolicella (corvina, molinara and rodinella) stand up to the richness of the Bolognese (About $13)

INDEX

Index

Note Boldfaced page numbers indicate photographs.

A

Artichokes

Chicken Scaloppine in an Artichoke Broth, 60, **78**

Pork Pot Roast with Artichoke & Peppers, 107

Spicy Shrimp and Bean Stew with Artichokes and Basil, 193

Tubettini Artichoke Bolognese, 228, 229

Arugula and Fresh Fig Salad, Chicken Breast with, 59, **79**

Asparagus

Spaghetti and Shrimp with Spring Vegetables, 175, **180**

Warm Shrimp and Asparagus Salad with Lemon Mayonnaise, 194

Avocados

Curried Salmon Salad with Avocado Relish, 144, **179**

Grilled Chicken with Avocado Relish, 57

prepping, 11

B

Bacon

Crispy Fried Shrimp with Warm Coleslaw, 165, **183**

Grilled Tuna Steak with Warm Bacon & Green Pea Salad, 152

Tiny Shrimp, Bacon, and Parsnip Casserole, 196

Warm Chicken & Bacon Salad, 88

Beans

Beef and Mushroom Chili, 41

Crispy Pork Chops with Rice & Beans, 118

Grilled Pork Chops & Beans, 108

Lamb Chops with Tiny White Beans & Raisins, 127

Puffy Chicken with White Beans & Curry, 82, **178**

Quick Chicken Stew with Tomatoes and Mustard, 87

Salmon with Lima Beans & Basil, 137

Shrimp Parmigiano with White Beans and Olives, 168

Spicy Shrimp and Bean Stew with Artichokes and Basil, 193

Stuffed Chicken Breasts with Giant White Beans, 81

Beef

Beef, Miso, and Shiitake Stir-Fry, 39

Beef and Crispy Potatoes with Blue Cheese, 40, **66**

Beef and Fried-Pepper Carpaccio, 29

Beef and Goat Cheese Raviolos, 44, **67**

Beef and Mushroom Chili, 41

Beef and Potato Gratin, 42

Beef and Snow Pea Quick Fry, 37

Beef Minute Steak with Sour Cherry-Mustard Glaze, 20

Beef Pot Roast with Cauliflower and Gravy, 46

Boiled Beef and Pappardelle, 32, **71**

Charred Steak with Mushroom Vinaigrette, 31

Chipped Beef with Rice Noodles and Chiles, 33

Cold Beef and Italian Bread Salad, 35

Filet Mignon with Cheese and Potatoes, 19

Flank Steak Forestiére, 25, **70**

Fried Beef with Broccoli and Garlic Sauce, 38

Grilled Beef Kabobs with Eggplant and Orzo, 30

Grilled Boneless Sirloin Diane, 208

Ground Beef and Gnocchi Pie, 43

Horseradish-and-Cinnamon-Marinated Skirt Steak with Pears and Scallions, 23, **69**

Hot and Sour Beef and Cabbage, 36

how to butterfly, 213

London broil, slicing, 12

Marmalade-Marinated Flank Steak with Glazed Carrots, 24

Meatloaf with Fried Onions and Tomato Gravy, **80**, 210-211

Medallions of Beef with Crab and Squash Stew, 27

Medallions of Beef with Gingered Greens, 26

Pepper Steak in a Flash, 22

Quick Beef and Mushroom Stew, 34

Roast Beef with Figs and Black Pepper, 47

Sautéed Beef with Spicy Sweet Potato Fries, 45, **77**

Sirloin Steak with Kale and Mustard, 21

Tenderloin of Beef with Bacon, Squash, and Five-Spice Powder, 28

Beets

Curried Salmon with Beet Tartar Salad, 136

Curried Turkey Fricassee, 95

Pork Burgers with Walnuts and Chow Chow, **76**, 112

Quick Lamb Stew with Sweet Red Wine Sauce, 129

Shrimp with Beets and Butter Lettuce, 170

Black-Eyed Peas, Turnip Greens, and Fresh Cranberry Relish, Pork Chops with, 117

Bread, Italian, and Cold Beef Salad, 35

Broccoli

Fried Beef with Broccoli and Garlic Sauce, 38

Salmon with Crunchy Broccoli & Lemon Butter, 135

Sweet and Sticky Coconut Shrimp, 169

Broccoli Rabe

Medallions of Beef with Gingered Greens, 26

Shrimp and Cherry Tomatoes, 166

Burgers, Pork, with Walnuts and Chow Chow, **76**, 112

C

Cabbage

Buttermilk-Battered Fried Chicken with Mashed Potatoes and Cabbage, 86

Crispy Fried Shrimp with Warm Coleslaw, 165, **183**

Hot and Sour Beef and Cabbage, 36

Steamed Salmon in Napa Cabbage, 142

Sweet and Sour Red Cabbage, 217

Tuna Steaks with Red Cabbage Slaw, 157

Carrots

Broiled Tuna with Warm Olive & Carrot Vinaigrette, 149, **191**

Caramelized Lamb Chops with Carrot & Mushroom Stew, 123

cutting on a bias, 12

Marmalade-Marinated Flank Steak with Glazed Carrots, 24

Cauliflower

Beef Pot Roast with Cauliflower and Gravy, 46

Chicken Breasts with Cauliflower and Citrus, **67**, 83

Chicken & Cauliflower Under a Brick, 53

Curried Turkey Fricassee, 95

Cheese

Beef and Crispy Potatoes with Blue Cheese, 40, **66**

Beef and Goat Cheese Raviolos, 44, **67**

Beef and Potato Gratin, 42

Chicken Cutlets with Goat Cheese-Scalloped Potatoes, 51

Chicken-Fried Turkey Steak with Walnut & Ricotta Gravy, 93

Cold Beef and Italian Bread Salad, 35

Creamy Parmesan Risotto with Chicken & Mushrooms, 91

Filet Mignon with Cheese and Potatoes, 19

Ground Beef and Gnocchi Pie, 43

Molten Chicken Cutlets with Kale, 62

Pan-Fried Swiss Chicken Bundles, 63

Pappardelle with Portobellos and Pecorino, 227

Pork Chops Stuffed with Portobello Mushrooms, 110

Shrimp Parmigiano with White Beans and Olives, 168

Tuna and Potatoes alla Mama, 161

Cherry, Sour, Mustard Glaze, Beef Minute Steak with, 20

Chicken

breasts, creating cutlets from, 11

Buttermilk-Battered Fried Chicken with Mashed Potatoes and Cabbage, 86

Chicken and Wild Mushroom Marsala, 52

Chicken Braised with Paprika & Dijon, 92

Chicken Breasts with Cauliflower and Citrus, **67**, 83

Chicken Breast with Fresh Fig and Arugula Salad, 59, **79**

Chicken & Cauliflower Under a Brick, 53

Chicken Cutlets with Goat Cheese-Scalloped Potatoes, 51

Chicken Kabobs in Hoisin with Grilled Corn, 58

Chicken Scaloppine in an Artichoke Broth, 60, **78**

Chicken Scaloppine with Potato Pancakes and Port Sauce, 61

Chicken with Garlic & Spaghetti, 90

Chicken with Lemon Butter, Thyme & Pimientos, 84

Chicken with Turmeric & Onions, **72**, 85

Creamy Parmesan Risotto with Chicken & Mushrooms, 91

Grilled Chicken Breast with Lemon, Pea, and Mint Potatoes, 56

Grilled Chicken with Avocado Relish, 57

Grilled Stuffed Chicken with Prosciutto and Peppers, 54

how to butterfly, 213

Marinated Fried Chicken with Herbs, 55

Molten Chicken Cutlets with Kale, 62

Pan-Fried Swiss Chicken Bundles, 63

Pan-Roasted Chicken Breast with Pickled Peppers, 64

Perfect Roasted Chicken Smothered in Caramelized Onions, **73**, 214-215

Puffy Chicken with White Beans & Curry, 82, **178**

Quick Chicken Stew with Tomatoes and Mustard, 87

Red Ginger Chicken Satay, 89

Stuffed Chicken Breasts with Giant White Beans, 81

Warm Chicken & Bacon Salad, 88

Chicory, Curried Grilled Lamb Chops with, 124

Chili, Beef and Mushroom, 41

Chives, mincing, 11

Clams

Clams with Scallions, Nori, and Sesame, 222

John Dory with a Ragout of Dill and Littleneck Clams, 218-219

Linguini with Clams, 223

Tuna with Clams, Mushrooms & Andouille Sausage, 160, **186**

Coconut Shrimp, Sweet and Sticky, 169

Condiments, 9

Corn, Grilled, Chicken Kabobs in Hoisin with, 58

Crab

Crab-Stuffed Tuna with Spinach, 151

Medallions of Beef with Crab and Squash Stew, 27

Soft Shell Crabs with XO Sauce, 221

Cranberry Relish, Fresh, Turnip Greens, and Black-Eyed Peas, Pork Chops with, 117

Cucumbers

Open-Faced Lamb Sandwich with Cucumber Raita, **74**, 130

Red Ginger Chicken Satay, 89

Thai Salmon Saté, 143

Curried dishes

Curried Grilled Lamb Chops with Chicory, 124

Curried Salmon Salad with Avocado Relish, 144, **179**

Curried Salmon with Beet Tartar Salad, 136

Curried Turkey Fricassee, 95

Puffy Chicken with White Beans & Curry, 82, **178**

D

Duck, Holiday, No-Brainer, 216-217

E

Eggplant

Grilled Beef Kabobs with Eggplant and Orzo, 30

Grilled Lamb with Sweet and Sour Eggplant, 126

Endive

Pork Medallions with Apricot & Endive, 116, **65**

Salmon Cooked in Salt with Sweet & Sour Endive, 141

Index

Entertaining, tips for, 203

Escarole, Turkey & Prosciutto Rolls with, 96

F

Fennel

Fennel Stuffed Loin of Pork, 212

Shrimp and Fennel Stew, 176

Figs

Chicken Breast with Fresh Fig and Arugula Salad, 59, **79**

Roast Beef with Figs and Black Pepper, 47

Fish. See also Salmon; Tuna

how to butterfly, 213

John Dory with a Ragout of Dill and Littleneck Clams, 218-219

G

Garlic

Fried Beef with Broccoli and Garlic Sauce, 38

prepping, 12

Ginger

Medallions of Beef with Gingered Greens, 26

Red Ginger Chicken Satay, 89

Gnocchi and Ground Beef Pie, 43

Greens

Crab-Stuffed Tuna with Spinach, 151

Curried Grilled Lamb Chops with Chicory, 124

Fried Pork Cutlets with Chopped Salad, 102

Grilled Pork Chops with Miso & Apple Dressing, 105

Jumbo Shrimp and Red Swiss Chard, 167

Medallions of Beef with Gingered Greens, 26

Miso Marmalade Salmon with Swiss Chard, 139

Molten Chicken Cutlets with Kale, 62

Orange and Cinnamon-Glazed Pork Tenderloin, 101

Pork Chops with Turnip Greens, Black-Eyed Peas, and Fresh Cranberry Relish, 117

Shrimp and Cherry Tomatoes, 166

Shrimp with Beets and Butter Lettuce, 170

Sirloin Steak with Kale and Mustard, 21

Turkey & Prosciutto Rolls with Escarole, 96

Grilled dishes

Beef Minute Steak with Sour Cherry-Mustard Glaze, 20

Broiled Salmon with Turnip & Onion Relish, 145

Broiled Tuna with Warm Olive & Carrot Vinaigrette, 149, **191**

Chicken Kabobs in Hoisin with Grilled Corn, 58

Cinnamon-Rubbed Grilled Lamb Chops with Sweet Potatoes, **75**, 131

Curried Grilled Lamb Chops with Chicory, 124

Curried Salmon with Beet Tartar Salad, 136

Grilled Baby Lamb Chops & Heirloom Tomatoes, 125

Grilled Beef Kabobs with Eggplant and Orzo, 30

Grilled Boneless Sirloin Diane, 208

Grilled Chicken Breast with Lemon, Pea, and Mint Potatoes, 56

Grilled Chicken with Avocado Relish, 57

Grilled Lamb with Sweet and Sour Eggplant, 126

Grilled Pork Chops and Peppers alla Brace, 104, **68**

Grilled Pork Chops & Beans, 108

Grilled Pork Chops with Cumin-Scented Fricassee of Tomatoes, 111

Grilled Pork Chops with Miso & Apple Dressing, 105

Grilled Pork with Cherry Tomatoes & Mustard, 109

Grilled Stuffed Chicken with Prosciutto and Peppers, 54

Grilled Tuna Steaks with Fresh Salsa Verde, 153

Grilled Tuna Steaks with Sweet & Sour Mangoes, 150

Grilled Tuna Steak with Warm Bacon & Green Pea Salad, 152

Horseradish-and-Cinnamon-Marinated Skirt Steak with Pears and Scallions, 23, **69**

Marmalade-Marinated Flank Steak with Glazed Carrots, 24

Open-Faced Lamb Sandwich with Cucumber Raita, **74**, 130

PorkChops Puttanesca, 106

Pork Chops with Turnip Greens, Black-Eyed Peas, and Fresh Cranberry Relish, 117

Pork Kabobs with Rosemary-Prune Glaze, 114

Pork Medallions with Apricot & Endive, 116, **65**

Red Ginger Chicken Satay, 89

Shrimp Scampi over Grilled Tomatoes, 172

Sweet & Sour Tuna, 155

Thai Salmon Saté, 143

Tuna Steaks with Red Cabbage Slaw, 157

Turkey & Prosciutto Rolls with Escarole, 96

Grill pans, using, 14

H

Ham. See Prosciutto

Horseradish-and-Cinnamon-Marinated Skirt Steak with Pears and Scallions, 23, **69**

I

Ingredients, 7, 9

J

John Dory with a Ragout of Dill and Littleneck Clams, 218-219

K

Kale

Molten Chicken Cutlets with Kale, 62

Sirloin Steak with Kale and Mustard, 21

L

Lamb

Caramelized Lamb Chops with Carrot & Mushroom Stew, 123

Cinnamon-Rubbed Grilled Lamb Chops with Sweet Potatoes, **75**, 131

Curried Grilled Lamb Chops with Chicory, 124

Grilled Baby Lamb Chops & Heirloom Tomatoes, 125

Grilled Lamb with Sweet and Sour Eggplant, 126

how to butterfly, 213

Lamb Chops with Tiny White Beans & Raisins, 127

Loin Lamb Chops alla Pizzaiolo, 128

Open-Faced Lamb Sandwich with Cucumber Raita, **74**, 130

Quick Lamb Stew with Sweet Red Wine Sauce, 129

Slow-Roasted Leg of Lamb, 209

Lettuce, Butter, and Beets, Shrimp with, 170

M

Beef

Beef, Miso, and Shiitake Stir-Fry, 39

Beef and Crispy Potatoes with Blue Cheese, 40, 66

Beef and Fried-Pepper Carpaccio, 29

Beef and Goat Cheese Raviolos, 44, **67**

Beef and Mushroom Chili, 41

Beef and Potato Gratin, 42

Beef and Snow Pea Quick Fry, 37

Beef Minute Steak with Sour Cherry-Mustard Glaze, 20

Beef Pot Roast with Cauliflower and Gravy, 46

Boiled Beef and Pappardelle, 32, **71**

Charred Steak with Mushroom Vinaigrette, 31

Chipped Beef with Rice Noodles and Chilies, 33

Cold Beef and Italian Bread Salad, 35

Filet Mignon with Cheese and Potatoes, 19

Flank Steak Forestière, 25, 70

Fried Beef with Broccoli and Garlic Sauce, 38

Grilled Beef Kabobs with Eggplant and Orzo, 30

Grilled Boneless Sirloin Diane, 208

Ground Beef and Gnocchi Pie, 43

Horseradish-and-Cinnamon-Marinated Skirt Steak with Pears and Scallions, 23, **69**

Hot and Sour Beef and Cabbage, 36

Marmalade-Marinated Flank Steak with Glazed Carrots, 24

Meatloaf with Fried Onions and Tomato Gravy, **80**, 210-211

Medallions of Beef with Crab and Squash Stew, 27

Medallions of Beef with Gingered Greens, 26

Pepper Steak in a Flash, 22

Quick Beef and Mushroom Stew, 34

Roast Beef with Figs and Black Pepper, 47

Sautéed Beef with Spicy Sweet Potato Fries, 45, **77**

Sirloin Steak with Kale and Mustard, 21

Tenderloin of Beef with Bacon, Squash, and Five-Spice Powder, 28

Fish

Broiled Salmon with Turnip & Onion Relish, 145

Broiled Tuna with Warm Olive & Carrot Vinaigrette, 149, **191**

Crab-Stuffed Tuna with Spinach, 151

Curried Salmon Salad with Avocado Relish, 144, **179**

Curried Salmon with Beet Tartar Salad, 136

Grilled Tuna Steaks with Fresh Salsa Verde, 153

Grilled Tuna Steaks with Sweet & Sour Mangoes, 150

Grilled Tuna Steak with Warm Bacon & Green Pea Salad, 152

John Dory with a Ragout of Dill and Littleneck Clams, 218-219

Miso Marmalade Salmon with Swiss Chard, 139

Salmon Cooked in Salt with Sweet & Sour Endive, 141

Salmon with Crunchy Broccoli & Lemon Butter, 135

Salmon with Lima Beans & Basil, 137

Sautéed Summer Roll of Salmon with Basil Pesto, 140, **188**

Seared & Sliced Tuna with Radishes & Snow Peas, 154, **187**

Steamed Salmon in Napa Cabbage, 142

Sweet & Sour Tuna, 155

Tea-Smoked Salmon Fillet with Sweet & Sour Potato Salad, 138

Thai Salmon Saté, 143

Tuna and Potatoes alla Mama, 161

Tuna Steaks with Red Cabbage Slaw, 157

Tuna & Tomatoes Poached in Olive Oil, 159

Tuna & Tomatoes with Creamy Polenta, 156

Tuna with Clams, Mushrooms & Andouille Sausage, 160, **186**

Tuna with Lemon, Capers & Parsley, 158

Main dishes - lamb

Caramelized Lamb Chops with Carrot & Mushroom Stew, 123

Cinnamon-Rubbed Grilled Lamb Chops with Sweet Potatoes, **75**, 131

Curried Grilled Lamb Chops with Chicory, 124

Grilled Baby Lamb Chops & Heirloom Tomatoes, 125

Grilled Lamb with Sweet and Sour Eggplant, 126

Lamb Chops with Tiny White Beans & Raisins, 127

Loin Lamb Chops 'alla Pizzaiolo,' 128

Open-Faced Lamb Sandwich with Cucumber Raita, **74**, 130

Quick Lamb Stew with Sweet Red Wine Sauce, 129

Slow-Roasted Leg of Lamb, 209

Pasta

Gnocchi with Veal and Porcini Ragu, 224-225

Pappardelle with Portobellos and Pecorino, 227

Spaghetti Scarpariello, 226

Tubettini Artichoke Bolognese, 228-229

Pork

Crispy Pork Chops with Rice & Beans, 118

Fennel Stuffed Loin of Pork, 212

Fried Pork Cutlets with Chopped Salad, 102

Grilled Pork Chops and Peppers alla Brace, 104, **68**

Grilled Pork Chops & Beans, 108

Grilled Pork Chops with Cumin-Scented Fricassee of Tomatoes, 111

Grilled Pork Chops with Miso & Apple Dressing, 105

Index

Grilled Pork with Cherry Tomatoes & Mustard, 109

Mexican Pork with Okra, 103

Orange and Cinnamon-Glazed Pork Tenderloin, 101

Pork Burgers with Walnuts and Chow Chow, **76**, 112

Pork Chops Stuffed with Portobello Mushrooms, 110

Pork Chops with Potatoes, 113

Pork Chops with Turnip Greens, Black-Eyed Peas, and Fresh Cranberry Relish, 117

Pork Kabobs with Rosemary-Prune Glaze, 114

Pork Medallions with Apricot & Endive, 116, **65**

Pork Medallions with Shrimp and Penne Primavera, 115

Pork Pot Roast with Artichoke & Peppers, 107

Sausage, Peppers & Tomatoes with Fennel Seed, 119

Main dishes - poultry

Buttermilk-Battered Fried Chicken with Mashed Potatoes and Cabbage, 86

Chicken and Wild Mushroom Marsala, 52

Chicken Braised with Paprika & Dijon, 92

Chicken Breasts with Cauliflower and Citrus, **67**, 83

Chicken Breast with Fresh Fig and Arugula Salad, 59, **79**

Chicken & Cauliflower Under a Brick, 53

Chicken Cutlets with Goat Cheese-Scalloped Potatoes, 51

Chicken-Fried Turkey Steak with Walnut & Ricotta Gravy, 93

Chicken Kabobs in Hoisin with Grilled Corn, 58

Chicken Scaloppine in an Artichoke Broth, 60, **78**

Chicken Scaloppine with Potato Pancakes and Port Sauce, 61

Chicken with Garlic & Spaghetti, 90

Chicken with Lemon Butter, Thyme & Pimientos, 84

Chicken with Turmeric & Onions, **72**, 85

Chopped Turkey Steaks, Italian-Style, 94

Creamy Parmesan Risotto with Chicken & Mushrooms, 91

Curried Turkey Fricassee, 95

Grilled Chicken Breast with Lemon, Pea, and Mint Potatoes, 56

Grilled Chicken with Avocado Relish, 57

Grilled Stuffed Chicken with Prosciutto and Peppers, 54

Marinated Fried Chicken with Herbs, 55

Molten Chicken Cutlets with Kale, 62

No-Brainer Holiday Duck, 216-217

Pan-Fried Swiss Chicken Bundles, 63

Pan-Roasted Chicken Breast with Pickled Peppers, 64

Perfect Roasted Chicken Smothered in Caramelized Onions, **73**, 214-215

Puffy Chicken with White Beans & Curry, 82, **178**

Quick Chicken Stew with Tomatoes and Mustard, 87

Red Ginger Chicken Satay, 89

Stuffed Chicken Breasts with Giant White Beans, 81

Turkey Breasts with Apricot & Grapefruit Glaze, 97

Turkey & Prosciutto Rolls with Escarole, 96

Warm Chicken & Bacon Salad, 88

Shellfish

Clams with Scallions, Nori, and Sesame, 222

Crispy Fried Shrimp with Warm Coleslaw, 165, **182**

Fried Scallops with Melted Onions, **184**, 197

John Dory with a Ragout of Dill and Littleneck Clams, 218-219

Jumbo Shrimp and Red Swiss Chard, 167

Jumbo Shrimp with Hot and Sour Honey Glaze, 171

Linguini with Clams, 223

Mama's Shrimp with Rice and Peppers, 195

Scallops with Burnt Onions and Lemon Butter, 199

Scallops with Mango Relish on Zucchini Cakes, 198

Shrimp and Cherry Tomatoes, 166

Shrimp and Fennel Stew, 176

Shrimp and Red Onion Pie, 173, **190**

Shrimp Pappardelle with Smoky Peppers, 174

Shrimp Parmigiano with White Beans and Olives, 168

Shrimp Scampi over Grilled Tomatoes, 172

Shrimp with Beets and Butter Lettuce, 170

Soft Shell Crabs with XO Sauce, 221

Spaghetti and Shrimp with Spring Vegetables, 175, **180**

Spicy Shrimp and Bean Stew with Artichokes and Basil, 193

Sweet and Sticky Coconut Shrimp, 169

Tiny Shrimp, Bacon, and Parsnip Casserole, 196

Warm Shrimp and Asparagus Salad with Lemon Mayonnaise, 194

Mangoes

Grilled Tuna Steaks with Sweet & Sour Mangoes, 150

Scallops with Mango Relish on Zucchini Cakes, 198

Marmalade-Marinated Flank Steak with Glazed Carrots, 24

Meat. See also Beef; Lamb; Pork; Veal

doneness levels, 15

testing doneness of, 15

Meatloaf with Fried Onions and Tomato Gravy, **80**, 210-211

Miso

Beef, Miso, and Shiitake Stir-Fry, 39

Grilled Pork Chops with Miso & Apple Dressing, 105

Miso Marmalade Salmon with Swiss Chard, 139

Mushrooms

Beef, Miso, and Shiitake Stir-Fry, 39

Beef and Mushroom Chili, 41

Caramelized Lamb Chops with Carrot & Mushroom Stew, 123

Charred Steak with Mushroom Vinaigrette, 31

Chicken and Wild Mushroom Marsala, 52

Creamy Parmesan Risotto with Chicken & Mushrooms, 91

Flank Steak Forestière, 25, **70**

Gnocchi with Veal and Porcini Ragu, 224-225

Grilled Boneless Sirloin Diane, 208

Pappardelle with Portobellos and Pecorino, 227

Pork Chops Stuffed with Portobello Mushrooms, 110

Quick Beef and Mushroom Stew, 34

Tuna with Clams, Mushrooms & Andouille Sausage, 160, **186**

N

Noodles

Chipped Beef with Rice Noodles and Chiles, 33

Puffy Chicken with White Beans & Curry, 82, **178**

Nuts. See Walnuts

O

Oil, heating, 13

Oils, types of, 9

Okra, Mexican Pork with, 103

Olives

Broiled Tuna with Warm Olive & Carrot Vinaigrette, 149, **191**

Pork Chops Puttanesca, 106

Shrimp Parmigiano with White Beans and Olives, 168

Spaghetti Scarpariello, 226

Onions

Broiled Salmon with Turnip & Onion Relish, 145

Chicken with Turmeric & Onions, 72, **85**

Fried Scallops with Melted Onions, **184**, 197

Meatloaf with Fried Onions and Tomato Gravy, **80**, 210-211

Perfect Roasted Chicken Smothered in Caramelized Onions, **73**, 214-215

Scallops with Burnt Onions and Lemon Butter, 199

Shrimp and Red Onion Pie, 173, **190**

sweating, 13

Orzo and Eggplant, Grilled Beef Kabobs with, 30

P

Pantry items, 7, 9

Parsley, chopping, 12

Parsnip, Tiny Shrimp, and Bacon Casserole, 196

Pasta. See also Noodles

Beef and Goat Cheese Raviolos, 44, **67**

Boiled Beef and Pappardelle, 32, **71**

Chicken with Garlic & Spaghetti, 90

Gnocchi with Veal and Porcini Ragu, 224-225

Grilled Beef Kabobs with Eggplant and Orzo, 30

Linguini with Clams, 223

Pappardelle with Portobellos and Pecorino, 227

Shrimp Pappardelle with Smoky Peppers, 174

Spaghetti and Shrimp with Spring Vegetables, 175, **180**

Spaghetti Scarpariello, 226

Tubettini Artichoke Bolognese, 228-229

Pears and Scallions, Horseradish-and-Cinnamon-Marinated Skirt Steak with, 23, **69**

Peas

Beef and Snow Pea Quick Fry, 37

Chicken with Garlic & Spaghetti, 90

Grilled Chicken Breast with Lemon, Pea, and Mint Potatoes, 56

Grilled Tuna Steak with Warm Bacon & Green Pea Salad, 152

Seared & Sliced Tuna with Radishes & Snow Peas, 154, **187**

Peppers

Beef and Fried-Pepper Carpaccio, 29

Chicken with Lemon Butter, Thyme & Pimientos, 84

Grilled Pork Chops and Peppers "Alla Brace," 104. **68**

Grilled Stuffed Chicken with Prosciutto and Peppers, 54

Jumbo Shrimp with Hot and Sour Honey Glaze, 171

Loin Lamb Chops 'alla Pizzaiolo,' 128

Mama's Shrimp with Rice and Peppers, 195

Pan-Roasted Chicken Breast with Pickled Peppers, 64

Pepper Steak in a Flash, 22

Pork Pot Roast with Artichoke & Peppers, 107

Sausage, Peppers & Tomatoes with Fennel Seed, 119

Shrimp Pappardelle with Smoky Peppers, 174

Pie, Shrimp and Red Onion, 173, **190**

Polenta

Tuna & Tomatoes with Creamy Polenta, 156

Pork. See also Bacon; Prosciutto

Crispy Pork Chops with Rice & Beans, 118

Fennel Stuffed Loin of Pork, 212

Fried Pork Cutlets with Chopped Salad, 102

Grilled Pork Chops and Peppers alla Brace, 104, **68**

Grilled Pork Chops & Beans, 108

Grilled Pork Chops with Cumin-Scented Fricassee of Tomatoes, 111

Grilled Pork Chops with Miso & Apple Dressing, 105

Grilled Pork with Cherry Tomatoes & Mustard, 109

how to butterfly, 213

Meatloaf with Fried Onions and Tomato Gravy, **80**, 210-211

Mexican Pork with Okra, 103

Orange and Cinnamon-Glazed Pork Tenderloin, 101

Pork Burgers with Walnuts and Chow Chow, **76**, 112

Pork Chops Puttanesca, 106, **77**

Pork Chops Stuffed with Portobello Mushrooms, 110

Pork Chops with Potatoes, 113

Pork Chops with Turnip Greens, Black-Eyed Peas, and Fresh Cranberry Relish, 117

Pork Kabobs with Rosemary-Prune Glaze, 114

Pork Medallions with Apricot & Endive, 116, **65**

Index

Pork Pot Roast with Artichoke & Peppers, 107

Sausage, Peppers & Tomatoes with Fennel Seed, 119

Tubettini Artichoke Bolognese, 228-229

Tuna with Clams, Mushrooms & Andouille Sausage, 160, **186**

Potatoes

Beef and Crispy Potatoes with Blue Cheese, 40, **66**

Beef and Potato Gratin, 42

Buttermilk-Battered Fried Chicken with Mashed Potatoes and Cabbage, 86

Chicken Cutlets with Goat Cheese-Scalloped Potatoes, 51

Chicken Scaloppine in an Artichoke Broth, 60, **78**

Chicken Scaloppine with Potato Pancakes and Port Sauce, 61

Cinnamon-Rubbed Grilled Lamb Chops with Sweet Potatoes, **75**, 131

Filet Mignon with Cheese and Potatoes, 19

Gnocchi with Veal and Porcini Ragu, 224-225

Grilled Chicken Breast with Lemon, Pea, and Mint Potatoes, 56

Loin Lamb Chops alla Pizzaiolo, 128

Luxurious Potato Purée, 220

Pork Chops with Potatoes, 113

Sautéed Beef with Spicy Sweet Potato Fries, 45, **77**

Seared & Sliced Tuna with Radishes & Snow Peas, 154, **187**

Tea-Smoked Salmon Fillet with Sweet & Sour Potato Salad, 138

Tuna and Potatoes alla Mama, 161

Poultry. See Chicken; Duck; Turkey

Prosciutto

Grilled Stuffed Chicken with Prosciutto and Peppers, 54

Turkey & Prosciutto Rolls with Escarole, 96

Prune-Rosemary Glaze, Pork Kabobs with, 114

Q

Quince and Grenadine Lacquer, 216-217

R

Radicchio

Fried Pork Cutlets with Chopped Salad, 102

Orange and Cinnamon-Glazed Pork Tenderloin, 101

Radishes

Seared & Sliced Tuna with Radishes & Snow Peas, 154, **187**

Sweet & Sour Tuna, 155

Raviolos, Beef and Goat Cheese, 44, **67**

Rice

Creamy Parmesan Risotto with Chicken & Mushrooms, 91

Crispy Pork Chops with Rice & Beans, 118

Mama's Shrimp with Rice and Peppers, 195

Risotto, Creamy Parmesan, with Chicken & Mushrooms, 91

S

Salads

Cold Beef and Italian Bread Salad, 35

Curried Salmon Salad with Avocado Relish, 144, **179**

Grilled Pork Chops with Miso & Apple Dressing, 105

Warm Chicken & Bacon Salad, 88

Warm Shrimp and Asparagus Salad with Lemon Mayonnaise, 194

Salmon

Broiled Salmon with Turnip & Onion Relish, 145

Curried Salmon Salad with Avocado Relish, 144, **179**

Curried Salmon with Beet Tartar Salad, 136

Miso Marmalade Salmon with Swiss Chard, 139

Salmon Cooked in Salt with Sweet & Sour Endive, 141

Salmon with Crunchy Broccoli & Lemon Butter, 135

Salmon with Lima Beans & Basil, 137

Sautéed Summer Roll of Salmon with Basil Pesto, 140, **188**

Steamed Salmon in Napa Cabbage, 142

Tea-Smoked Salmon Fillet with Sweet & Sour Potato Salad, 138

Thai Salmon Saté, 143

Sandwich, Open-Faced Lamb, with Cucumber Raita, **74**, 130

Saté, Thai Salmon, 143

Sausages

Sausage, Peppers & Tomatoes with Fennel Seed, 119

Tubettini Artichoke Bolognese, 228-229

Tuna with Clams, Mushrooms & Andouille Sausage, 160, **186**

Scallions, Nori, and Sesame, Clams with, 222

Scallops

Fried Scallops with Melted Onions, **184**, 197

Scallops with Burnt Onions and Lemon Butter, 199

Scallops with Mango Relish on Zucchini Cakes, 198

Seasonings and spices, 9

Shellfish. See also Shrimp

Clams with Scallions, Nori, and Sesame, 222

Crab-Stuffed Tuna with Spinach, 151

Fried Scallops with Melted Onions, **184**, 197

John Dory with a Ragout of Dill and Littleneck Clams, 218-219

Linguini with Clams, 223

Medallions of Beef with Crab and Squash Stew, 27

Scallops with Burnt Onions and Lemon Butter, 199

Scallops with Mango Relish on Zucchini Cakes, 198

Soft Shell Crabs with XO Sauce, 221

Tuna with Clams, Mushrooms & Andouille Sausage, 160, **186**

Shrimp

Crispy Fried Shrimp with Warm Coleslaw, 165, **183**

Jumbo Shrimp and Red Swiss Chard, 167

Jumbo Shrimp with Hot and Sour Honey Glaze, 171

Mama's Shrimp with Rice and Peppers, 195

Shrimp and Cherry Tomatoes, 166

Shrimp and Fennel Stew, 176

Shrimp and Red Onion Pie, 173, **190**

Shrimp Pappardelle with Smoky Peppers, 174

Shrimp Parmigiano with White Beans and Olives, 168

Shrimp Scampi over Grilled Tomatoes, 172

Shrimp with Beets and Butter Lettuce, 170

Spaghetti and Shrimp with Spring Vegetables, 175, **180**

Spicy Shrimp and Bean Stew with Artichokes and Basil, 193

Sweet and Sticky Coconut Shrimp, 169

Tiny Shrimp, Bacon, and Parsnip Casserole, 196

Warm Shrimp and Asparagus Salad with Lemon Mayonnaise, 194

Soups

Boiled Beef and Pappardelle, 32, **71**

Spinach, Crab-Stuffed Tuna with, 151

Squash

Scallops with Mango Relish on Zucchini Cakes, 198

Tenderloin of Beef with Bacon, Squash, and Five-Spice Powder, 28

Stews

Curried Turkey Fricassee, 95

Quick Beef and Mushroom Stew, 34

Quick Chicken Stew with Tomatoes and Mustard, 87

Quick Lamb Stew with Sweet Red Wine Sauce, 129

Shrimp and Fennel Stew, 176

Spicy Shrimp and Bean Stew with Artichokes and Basil, 193

Stir-fries

Beef, Miso, and Shiitake Stir-Fry, 39

Beef and Crispy Potatoes with Blue Cheese, 40, **66**

Beef and Snow Pea Quick Fry, 37

Fried Beef with Broccoli and Garlic Sauce, 38

Hot and Sour Beef and Cabbage, 36

Summer Roll of Salmon, Sautéed, with Basil Pesto, 140, **188**

Sweeteners, 9

Sweet potatoes

Cinnamon-Rubbed Grilled Lamb Chops with Sweet Potatoes, **75**, 131

Sautéed Beef with Spicy Sweet Potato Fries, 45, **77**

Seared & Sliced Tuna with Radishes & Snow Peas, 154, **187**

Swiss chard

Jumbo Shrimp and Red Swiss Chard, 167

Miso Marmalade Salmon with Swiss Chard, 139

T

Techniques

avocados, prepping, 11

beef London broil, slicing, 12

chicken breasts, creating cutlets from, 11

chives, mincing, 11

cutting on a bias, 12

garlic, prepping, 12

grill pans, using, 14

meat, levels of doneness, 15

meat, testing doneness level, 15

oil heating, 13

onions, sweating, 13

parsley, chopping, 12

Tomatillos

Grilled Tuna Steaks with Fresh Salsa Verde, 153

Tomatoes

Grilled Baby Lamb Chops & Heirloom Tomatoes, 125

Grilled Pork Chops with Cumin-Scented Fricassee of Tomatoes, 111

Grilled Pork with Cherry Tomatoes & Mustard, 109

Meatloaf with Fried Onions and Tomato Gravy, **80**, 210-211

Quick Chicken Stew with Tomatoes and Mustard, 87

Shrimp and Cherry Tomatoes, 166

Shrimp Scampi over Grilled Tomatoes, 172

Spaghetti Scarpariello, 226

Tuna & Tomatoes Poached in Olive Oil, 159

Tuna & Tomatoes with Creamy Polenta, 156

Tuna

Broiled Tuna with Warm Olive & Carrot Vinaigrette, 149, **191**

Crab-Stuffed Tuna with Spinach, 151

Grilled Tuna Steaks with Fresh Salsa Verde, 153

Grilled Tuna Steaks with Sweet & Sour Mangoes, 150

Grilled Tuna Steak with Warm Bacon & Green Pea Salad, 152

Seared & Sliced Tuna with Radishes & Snow Peas, 154, **187**

Sweet & Sour Tuna, 155

Tuna and Potatoes alla Mama, 161

Tuna Steaks with Red Cabbage Slaw, 157

Tuna & Tomatoes Poached in Olive Oil, 159

Tuna & Tomatoes with Creamy Polenta, 156

Tuna with Clams, Mushrooms & Andouille Sausage, 160, **186**

Tuna with Lemon, Capers & Parsley, 158

Turkey

Chicken-Fried Turkey Steak with Walnut & Ricotta Gravy, 93

Chopped Turkey Steaks, Italian-Style, 94

Curried Turkey Fricassee, 95

Turkey Breasts with Apricot & Grapefruit Glaze, 97

Turkey & Prosciutto Rolls with Escarole, 96

Turnip & Onion Relish, Broiled Salmon with, 145

V

Veal and Porcini Ragu, Gnocchi with, 224-225

Vinegars, 9

W

Walnuts

Chicken-Fried Turkey Steak with Walnut & Ricotta Gravy, 93

Pork Burgers with Walnuts and Chow Chow, **76**, 112

Wine, guide to, 204-207

Z

Zucchini Cakes, Scallops with Mango Relish on, 198

Acknowledgments

For their love I would like to thank my family: Mama, Dad, Maria and Jack, Michael and Patti, Teesha and Pumpkin.

For her guidance, support, and patience: Linda Lisco.

The incomparable Michael "MAP" Pedicone because he doesn't really exist.

Every book has been a labor of love, and this one was no exception. I am so proud to be a part of the brilliant team at Meredith Books, both in New York and Iowa: Jan Miller, Mick Schnepf, Lisa Berkowitz, Lisa Kingsley, and Amy Nichols; Tricia Laning, Erin Burns, Robert Jacobs, Craig Matthews, Laura Hart, Blaine Moats, Charles Worthington, and Greg Scheideman.

Big thanks to:
My recipe testers, Ed Moon, Kerstie Howser and Kris Kurek—these recipes are really good, thanks to them!

Everyone at Bertolli: Jon Affleck, Jen Daly, Christine Cea, and Russell Lily.

The creative geniuses at MRM, McCann-Erickson, and Ogilvy & Mather—and especially Henry Corra and Laura Murphy.

Donyale McRae and Sherri Stinger.

My peeps at Moosylvania, Martini & Rossi, and Bacardi: Josh Hayes and Erica Thurston.

Jim Dowd and his crack team at The Dowd Agency.

Everyone at Greater Talent New York.

My friends at William Morris: Mark Itkin, Suzy Unger, Brooke Slavik, Carey Berman, Todd Jacobs, and Jeff Google.

The folks at Lincoln MKX, especially Missy Rush, Thomais Zaremba, and Joe Pitka.

The very talented people of The Today Show, Top Chef, and Bravo.

Nancy Dubuque, Rob Sharenow, Michael Morrison, and Andy Berg at A&E.

My TriBros: Geoffrey "Big Man" O'leary, Scott "Doc" Duke, Nick "Stretch" Amico, and Scott "Trikid" Cohen.

For the laughs: Alexis De Chimay, Jeff Dello Russo, Colin Cowie, Stuart Brownstein, Whitney Casey, Mike Figliola, Ben Silverman, Tracey Edmonds, Jackie Green, Angus McIndoe, Jeffrey Morrone, and Allan Wyse.

Family Guy and South Park for getting me through the night.

And most importantly, thanks to my readers, bloggers, and fellow good-life lovers. What motivates me in life is the desire to laugh hard and often—and without all of you that wouldn't be possible.